500
TERRIFIC
IDEAS
FOR
Home Maintenance and Repair

500
TERRIFIC
IDEAS
FOR
Home Maintenance and Repair

Jack Maguire

Galahad Books · New York

A Round Stone Press book.

Directors: Marsha Melnick, Paul Fargis, Susan E. Meyer
Design: Jeff Fitschen
Illustrations: Norm Nuding

Molly is a registered trademark of the Molly Fastener Group.
Lysol disinfectant is a registered trademark of Lehn & Fink Consumer Products.
Styrofoam is a registered trademark of Dow Chemical U.S.A.
Plexiglas is a registered trademark of Rohm & Haas Co.
Velcro is a registered trademark of Velcro U.S.A.

First Galahad Books edition published in 1997.

Galahad Books
A division of Budget Book Service, Inc.
386 Park Avenue South
New York, NY 10016

Galahad Books is a registered trademark of Budget Book Service, Inc.

Published by arrangement with Round Stone Press, Inc.

Library of Congress Catalog Card Number: 96-79816

ISBN: 0-88365-993-X

Printed in the United States of America.

Contents

INTRODUCTION

To own a home is to face ongoing repair and caretaking challenges. *500 Terrific Ideas for Home Maintenance and Repair* is a treasury of creative tips that will help you successfully meet these challenges. In each chapter you'll discover a wealth of suggestions for making home maintenance tasks easier, quicker, more effective, less expensive, and—most important of all—safer. Every entry is a concise, independent tip that can be readily grasped and assimilated into your own way of doing things. Altogether, the entries cover the full range of tasks that most homeowners have to manage—either routinely or on an emergency basis.

Because there are a number of different ways to execute any maintenance job, a variety of options are offered. You'll be able to make intelligent choices about what best fits your particular situation and style. In addition to using this book as a practical reference source, browse through it from time to time. You'll find it both instructive and entertaining.

The best general advice on taking care of a house is to plan ahead carefully for each task, which includes anticipating problems that may arise. Any forethought you give to setting up your workshop, tending your tools, and assessing the steps and resources needed for each job will be amply rewarded. No maintenance challenge is daunting if you break it down into parts and look at those parts with an open mind. Your personal ingenuity will inevitably rise to the occasion, and, over time, you will develop your own treasury of terrific ideas.

1

HOME WORKSHOP

1 Easy-to-find tools

A busy workshop is inevitably a cluttered workshop. The better you can see what lies around you, the safer and more efficient your work will be. For this reason, white is the best color for the walls, floor, and work surfaces. Use a semigloss paint. Its surface is much easier to wipe clean than flat paint, but does not create glare and reflections like a glossy surface.

2 Double-duty workbench top

A workbench with a hardwood top is ideal for withstanding wear and tear, but it's also very expensive. As an alternative top, nail tempered hardboard onto a sheet of ¾-inch plywood. Hardboard's tough, smooth surface makes wipe-up easy, while the plywood provides support. When the hardboard becomes worn, simply pull the nails out, turn the hardboard over, and nail it back again with the unused side facing up.

3 Workbench mat

Ironically, tools that are used and stored with the utmost care often get damaged when they're lying out on a hard, cluttered workbench. This is far less likely to happen if you keep a foam rubber mat or a piece of carpet remnant on your workbench specifically for parking your tools temporarily when you're not using them.

4 Fold-away workbench

If space is scarce in your workshop, build a fold-away workbench. Use a ¾ -inch plywood sheet or a solid-core door for the benchtop. Fasten the rear edge of the top directly to a wood-surface wall, or to a 2×3 cleat screwed to the wall studs. Use a continuous "piano" hinge so that the top can fold up out of the way and be held by a hook and screw eye at each side. Attach two blocks on the underside, near the front, to engage a frame that forms diagonal "legs." Hinge the leg frame to a cleat at the floor level that is the same thickness as the top, so the frame will fold flat against the folded top. Hold the frame in its folded-away position with a hook and eye, or a magnetic catch.

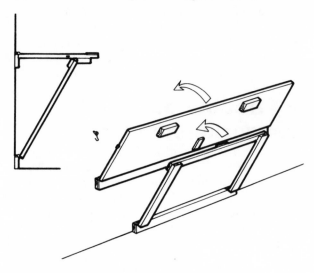

5 Padded floor

The typical workroom floor is concrete, which is not only hard on the feet but also hard on tools that are dropped. Make the floor more resilient with a vinyl sheet floor covering. Remnant lengths are available quite cheaply at floor covering stores.

6 Metal square hanger

A foot-long scrap of tongue-and-groove flooring or siding makes a great hanger for a large metal square. Just nail the scrap horizontally on the workshop wall with the groove side up. One blade of the square will fit into the groove while the other hangs down against the wall. If you don't have a tongue-and-groove scrap, clamp a board in your vise and cut a groove into one long edge with a hand or power saw, or run the board over your table saw.

7 File rug

Wood and metal files kept in a workbench drawer can shift around and damage each other every time you move the drawer. To prevent this, fit a piece of carpet into the bottom of the drawer.

8 Block that drawer

Don't run the risk of pulling a workbench drawer all the way out and spilling tools on your feet. Screw a vertical block of wood to the inside back of the drawer so it sticks up and will hit the facing at the front of the bench when the drawer is pulled out, thus preventing the drawer from going any further. If you ever need to take out the drawer, simply reach to the back and turn the block down, out of the way. An even simpler measure is to paint bright, highly visible lines inside the drawer at the point on the sides where it's advisable to stop pulling.

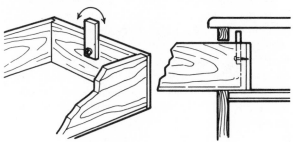

9 Foam-block organizer

Eliminate the clutter caused by drill bits, small knives, and punches on the top of your workbench or in a workbench drawer. Press all these items into a foot-long block of foam plastic that's been securely fastened to a surface near your workbench. Foam blocks are cheap and widely available at craft stores.

10 Wire-pinning

Many workbenches are cluttered with wires connected to different power tools. This situation is not only confusing, it's also dangerous. Get rid of the clutter by creating clothespin routing devices. Tack or bolt two or three rows of spring-type clothespins across the top of the wall facing your workbench and then use the clips of the clothespins to hold the wires. Different clothespins or clothespin rows can hold the wires for different tools.

11 Grounding a metal workbench

If your workbench is metal, be sure to ground it to a *cold* water pipe by linking the two securely together with conducting wire. This will prevent you from being shocked in the event that you're working with electrical equipment that develops a short and touches the bench.

12 Ring around the nuts and washers

To store nuts and washers so that they're easy to see and retrieve, hang them on large key rings or clip rings like those used to hang shower curtains. Look for rings with latches that are easy to manipulate and yet secure. Similar sized nuts or washers can be hung on the same ring, and the ring can be hung on a small towel rack with other rings or by itself on a perforated-board hook.

13 Extra storage space

If there's one thing a home workshop can always use, it's more storage space. Increase the storage space in your workshop by removing the plywood or wallboard between two studs. Nail horizontal boards between the studs to make shelves.

14 Organizing with a shoebag

A shoe bag on a wall or inside a closet door of your workshop makes an excellent place to store plastic bottles of shop liquids or cans of hardware. It keeps them from being knocked over and saves valuable shelf space.

15 Home-made hardware container

With a few strokes of a knife or a pair of scissors, a plastic bottle can be turned into an ideal container for small tools or hardware. Use gallon bottles for large-size containers; those used for antifreeze or laundry bleach are sturdier than milk bottles. Use quart-size bottles for small-item containers. Cut them as shown, retaining the handle on a large bottle. A plywood tray with 3-inch sides is a good way to keep several small containers together and to carry them to the job.

16 Hanging jars

Small glass jars with screw tops make perfect containers for nails, screws, nuts, and other small pieces of hardware. Unfortunately, they tend to take up a lot of storage room. Solve this problem by screwing the lids of the jars to the undersides of shelves. Then you can simply screw each jar into and out of its appropriate lid while the lid stays conveniently in place. Hang the jars where you can easily see the contents, and put a lock washer under the head of each screw so that the lid won't turn when you're twisting the attached jar.

17 Hardware samples

Why put up with the frustration and wasted time of opening one small box after another to find the right nail or screw for the job at hand? Attach a sample screw or nail to the outside with a rubber band or a dab of glue.

18 Sandpaper bagging

Many do-it-yourselfers don't realize that normal humidity changes can shorten the life of sandpaper, sanding belts, and other abrasive sheets. Store these items in zip-lock plastic bags or in sealed plastic containers to keep them dry.

19 Touch-tubes

Many glues, caulks, cements, and other adhesive substances are packaged in squeezable tubes that are sticky to handle and cumbersome to store; and all too easily the contents tend to lump up or dry out. The remedy lies in creating a line-up of hanging tubes that are ready to work when you are. Use a 3-inch-long piece of strong tape for each tube. Attach it to the bottom on one side, extending outward, and fold it back on itself, sticky faces together, to stick to the other side. This creates an extension tab about 2 inches long. Punch a small hole in this tab, and hang it on a nail or hook, next to other hanging tubes. The upside-down position insures that the contents will stay near the tip and will exit the tube cleanly and smoothly.

20 Glue cap replacement

When you lose a glue cap or the top of a glue tube splits, all is not lost. A screw-on wire cap, used to splice wires, makes a good replacement top that is easy to open and close. Keep a supply of various sizes of wire caps on hand for this and similar purposes.

21 Two-timing is real timing

How long will a job take? Carpenters, painters, wood-workers, and masons all offer this tip: Add up the hours or days it would take to do the job if every step went perfectly. Double that—because things won't go perfectly—and you'll be within 10 percent of the actual time it will take.

22 Toxic waste storage and disposal

The average workshop contains a surprising amount of toxic chemicals, such as solvents. For safety's sake, be sure to store these chemicals in a separate, sealed trash container or metal locker. Contact your local department of environmental protection to find out how and where to dispose of them.

23 File for manuals

Don't risk losing operator's manuals, warranties, bills of sale, and other important documents relating to the items in your home that may require repair or maintenance. Create a special file in your workshop to store these items. A metal file box with a flip-top lid and alphabetized cardboard dividers would be ideal for this purpose. A cardboard file box might not protect the stored documents from oil, grease, or paint damage. If you find it necessary to carry a manual or instruction sheet in your toolkit, protect it against dirt and grease with a clear plastic food storage bag.

24 Systematized job jars

A job jar is any receptacle—jar, basket, box, or can—that serves as a handyperson's suggestion box. Whenever any member of the household spots the need for a certain repair or maintenance task, he or she writes it down on a slip of paper and places it in the job jar so that it won't be forgotten. To help make this idea work effectively, set up three containers in a convenient place in your workshop or utility room, one labelled NOW for tasks that should be accomplished as soon as possible; one labeled SOON for tasks that have lower priority; and one labeled PLAN/BUY for tasks that require further study and/or the purchase of new materials before they can be tackled. Also, keep a pencil or pen and a good supply of paper next to your job jars and be sure to review their contents on a regular basis.

25 Storing plywood

Don't store sheets of plywood standing vertically or they may warp. Store them horizontally on overhead racks (with slats about a foot apart) in your workshop or garage, or on your attic floor.

26 Plan ahead

Don't begin a multistep workshop project without first writing down the steps on a sheet of paper and then posting the list on a clipboard hung in an easy-to-see spot on your workshop wall. Or, if you prefer, write the steps with a dry-erase, felt-tip marker on one of the smooth, white plastic memo or notice boards you can buy in an office supply store. The few minutes it takes to draw up these instructions is well spent, considering the time and effort you may waste if you do things out of sequence or if you forget steps and have to put the project on hold.

27 A ready-made parts tray

Many maintenance and repair jobs involve paying attention to the order in which you disassemble something composed of small parts. An empty egg carton can help you do this. Number the compartments with a marker, and as you work simply place each individual part, in sequence, into the appropriate compartment. That way, all the parts are ready, in reverse order, to be put back together again.

28 Ease the way with paraffin

Keep a block of paraffin wax in your workshop. Rub screws across it, and they will penetrate wood with less difficulty. You can also use paraffin to lubricate drawer guides, saw blades, drill bits, and the sole plates of electric tools so that they perform more smoothly and effectively. Paraffin is better than soap for these purposes because it does not attract atmospheric moisture that can rust metal.

29 Lagging it

Because of their relatively large diameter and large coarse threads, lag screws have a tendency to cause splits when used in soft woods. To avoid this, drill a full-depth pilot hole that is at least half the diameter of the screw threads.

30 Easier nailing

The holding power of a nail with a smooth shaft depends on friction between the shaft and the surrounding wood fibers. For this reason, do not wax nails or wipe them with linseed oil to make them easier to drive. Instead, especially in hardwoods, drill a pilot hole about half the diameter of the shaft.

31 A point well made

Too often sharpening a dull shop pencil with a utility knife results in a cut finger. Avoid this problem by taping a small square of medium-grit sandpaper to your workbench or a nearby spot on the wall. Rubbing the point of the pencil back and forth against the sandpaper gives you a sharp point quickly and painlessly.

32 Stick-less glue cap

Frequently the cap on a tube of glue or cement winds up sticking to the tube itself. Avoid this problem by applying a small amount of petroleum jelly to the threads before putting the cap back on.

33 Sharp trick with an old belt

Don't throw out an old leather belt just because it's lost its luster. Instead, cut off a 6-inch strip and glue it to a larger board. You can use it as a strop to finish the edge on sharpened knives, chisels, and other blades.

34 Handy clean-up

For hands covered with grease or paint, sawdust can work magic. While your hands are still wet, rub them with sawdust and watch them come clean before your eyes. It's safer, more convenient, and more economical than using a solvent or commercial cleaner.

35 Easy on your hands

Want to make it easier to get your hands clean after doing a messy repair or maintenance job? Before you even begin the job, rub your hands with liquid soap (no water). Wipe off any excess soap, but don't rinse. Then scratch a bar of solid soap with your finger-nails. The liquid soap will give your hands a thin dirt-repelling shield, while the soap caught under your nails will keep dirt from collecting there.

36 Thinner squirter

The next time you finish using a ketchup squeeze bottle with a flip-top lid, don't throw it out. Clean it thoroughly, remove the label, and use it to store paint thinner or any other liquid or semiliquid workshop substance. Whenever you need that substance, you can squirt exactly the amount you want with no fuss and no mess. To prevent potentially dangerous mix-ups, take care to mark the squirter's new contents clearly.

37 First aid for eyes

Keep a bottle of boric acid solution on a convenient shelf in your workshop, preferably a bottle with an eye-cup molded to the top. It makes a good eye rinse in case you get a bit of sawdust or dirt, or an irritating or harsh liquid in your eye. After rinsing, seek medical care. Also, note the expiration date for the solution (it typically lasts for about a year).

38 Broom stiffener

Natural bristle brooms wear down fast in a workroom, especially if the floor is concrete. Prolong the life of your natural bristle broom by dipping the bristles in a shallow container filled with thinned shellac. After the shellac dries, the bristles will be much stronger.

39 From paintbrush to dustbrush

An old paint brush that's too stiff or ragged for painting anymore can easily be turned into a handy dust brush for your workbench. Simply cut across the width of the bristles so that you have a smooth, slightly angled brushing surface (the angle-cut is useful in corners). When you're not using the brush, hang it on the wall or the side of your workbench by the hole in the handle.

2

TOOLS

40 A shop tool from your dentist

The next time you visit your dentist, ask if he or she has any old dental picks. They're good for marking and inscribing, as well as for cleaning, carving, and moving small pieces.

41 Bobby pin tweezer

Want to save your fingers from getting hurt when you're driving a nail? Use a bobby pin as a pair of miniature tweezers to hold the nail in place while you hammer. This is especially welcome when you're working with small nails.

42 Perfect putty-knife scraper

Every time you use a putty knife to apply putty, you have to deal with the problem of keeping the knife blade clean as you're working. To solve this problem neatly once and for all, make a scraper out of an old tin can. First, choose a can that's twice as high as the width of your knife blade. Cut a slit the same thickness as the knife blade down one side of the can, to a depth somewhat more than the blade width. To clean the knife, insert the blade into the slit at the handle and pull it toward you. The slit edges will scrape both sides of the blade clean and the putty will fall neatly into the can.

43 Extra leverage for your screwdriver

A bar-style can and bottle opener (the type with one rounded end for removing bottle caps and one pointed end for puncturing can tops) can easily be turned into a clever tool for giving your screwdriver more leverage. Simply cut a slit in the rounded end that is the right size to slide snugly around the tip of your screwdriver blade. Then cover the rest of the opener with tape to make it more comfortable for your hands. The result is a slotted wrench that can help you turn the tip of your screwdriver blade.

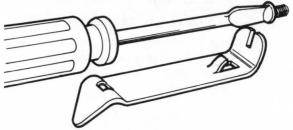

44 Hand-helping sponges

Don't throw away worn-out kitchen sponges. Instead, use them as hand-savers in the workshop. When you're using a metal file or a screwdriver, for example, a sponge wrapped around the tool can make it more comfortable to hold and can keep it from slipping if your hands perspire.

45 Humidity busters

Metal tools that sit unused in your toolbox for long periods of time risk getting rusty from the moisture in the air. A cone of carpenter's chalk or a charcoal briquette placed on the bottom of the toolbox acts as a perfect drying agent to prevent this from happening. When the carpenter's chalk feels damp, heat it in an oven at low temperature for 15 minutes to make it ready for use again. When the charcoal briquette feels damp, take it out and replace it with another.

46 Cord storage tubes

Keep tool cords and extension cords from tangling or getting in your way between jobs. Loop the cords loosely and slide them into cardboard tubes left over from rolls of paper towels, wax paper, or foil wrap.

47 Make-it-yourself pliers

When you need a kind of plier-wrench with long handles for extra leverage, you can make a very efficient tool out of two pieces of hardwood or two lengths of angle iron. One method is to simply bind them together at one end with loops of strong cord or wire. But a better method is illustrated. Drill holes and insert a length of chain through them; insert bolts or large nails through a link on each side to adjust the size of the opening between the "jaws." Slip jaws at this end on to the item to be turned, squeeze the handles together at the other end, and turn the tool like a wrench. For a better grip on a round object, such as a large pipe, wrap the object with a strip of scrap rubber or a layer of rubber electrical tape.

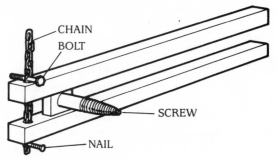

CHAIN
BOLT
SCREW
NAIL

48 A shavings fan

While operating a power drill, shavings often collect around the hole and prevent you from seeing what you're doing. The solution is a simple fan attached to the drill bit itself. Cut a strip from an old inner tube about ½ inch wide and 3 inches long. Then slit it twice in the middle near opposite edges. Insert the drill bit through the slits and slide the strip up to the top of the bit. When the bit rotates, the strip swirls like a propeller, blowing away all the shavings.

49 Spotlight on a drill

Many times you need extra light on a spot that you are drilling. Provide this extra light by taping a penlight to the drill. When you're finished, the penlight is easily removed.

50 On-target drilling

When you're drilling a hole on a curved or slick surface, take some precautions to keep the drill from sliding and causing damage. Center-punch the exact spot you want to drill, cover it with a piece of masking tape, and poke the tape into the punch mark with a sharp pencil or nail. Start drilling where the tape is poked; the bit will cut through the tape and into the punch mark without veering off to the side.

51 Lube job for drill bits

Want to make your drill bits last longer and stay sharper? Before each use, lubricate them with silicone spray. This will make them work more efficiently, thereby increasing the time it takes before they wear down or break.

52 Safe and tidy masonry drilling

Every time you drill into masonry, you risk losing control of the drill bit before it gets firmly lodged in place. To eliminate this risk, make a small wooden guide piece. Drill the same size hole you want in the masonry through the center of the guide piece. Before you drill, attach the guide with two or three spots of hot-melt glue to the masonry, directly over the target spot. After you drill, the guide piece will snap off with only a little prying and can be used again.

53 A notch-style drill jig

To start drilling at a perfectly vertical angle to a surface, use a jig consisting of a corner-notched 2×4. Place the inside corner of the notch directly over the spot where you want to drill, and align the drill bit snugly against the block. When you start the drill, it will go straight downward.

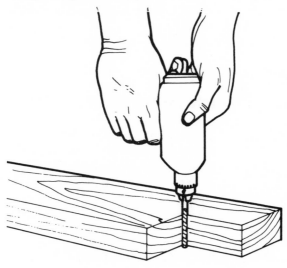

54 Sandwich-style drilling

To avoid rough or bent edges when drilling through metal, sandwich the metal between two thin scraps of wood and then drill through the entire sandwich. A variation of this same technique works for avoiding exit-hole splinters when drilling through plywood: Simply clamp a thin scrap of wood under the plywood and drill through into the scrap piece.

55 Retractable chuck key

A chuck key is easy to misplace. To keep it always handy by a bench- or stand-mounted power tool, clip it to a retractable key chain and attach the chain case securely to the body of the tool.

56 Filing soft metals

You don't have to avoid filing soft metals like brass or aluminum because they clog the file's teeth. The next time you want to file soft metals, simply rub a piece of chalk across the file before you begin. The metal debris left in the file can be easily cleaned out with a machinist's file "card," a fine, metal-toothed brush.

57 Cleaning your files

Cleaning small particles from between the teeth of a file doesn't have to be tedious. Just roll a ball of putty over the file and then pull it off. It will bring the particles along with it. Between cleanings, store the putty in a sealed jar. It can be revitalized with just a few drops of linseed oil.

58 Chisel in comfort

Chisel handles tend to be uncomfortable. To make chiseling easier on your hands, push a PVC pipe cap over the end of each chisel handle. If the cap doesn't fit snugly, wrap friction tape around the handle to increase its diameter, or glue the cap in place.

59 Kinder grip for chisel hammering

When you need to hammer a chisel, first wrap a thin sponge around the handle of the hammer. It will absorb some of the shock and make hammering easier on your hand and arm.

60 Super-scraper

Sometimes wood resists smooth planing or scraping because it's too hard, too full of knots, or the grain changes direction too often. Dealing with this kind of situation requires turning your plane into a super-scraper. Grind the front edge of an old plane iron at a bit more than 90 degrees to the work surface. Remove the edge burr on a leather strap or emery cloth. Mounted in a smooth plane, this scraper will produce a finely finished level surface with surprising ease.

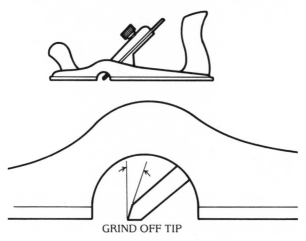

GRIND OFF TIP

61 A cleaner sander

The faceplate of a sander needs to be perfectly clean and flat so that the sanding disc mounted on top of it can perform its job effectively for a long period of time. Unfortunately, the old adhesive from a worn-out disc can be very difficult to remove. To make the task easier, wipe rubber cement thinner (available at office and art supply stores) on the adhesive and let it set for a few seconds until it softens. Then rub sawdust into the adhesive with a coarse rag, using broad, circular motions. The sawdust will collect the adhesive into small pellets that will brush right off.

62 Sanding block pads

Foam plastic trays, often used in meat packaging, make excellent sanding-block pads. First, cut a block of wood big enough to support about one-third of a sheet of sandpaper. Then glue a section of the foam tray to the wood. The foam cushion is resilient enough to prevent the "sandpaper" from tearing and strong enough to facilitate smooth sanding.

63 A handle with care

Sanding a small piece of metal or wood is often dangerous to the fingers. To protect them, temporarily attach the piece to the end of a dowel rod with hot-melt glue. When you've finished the job, put the whole thing in the freezer. The glue will dry out and the piece will automatically detach in just a few minutes.

64 Emery board sander

Keep a supply of emery boards on hand. They're very useful when you need to sand small pieces, or tiny cuts, or a surface that is difficult to reach.

65 Double-decker sawing

Whenever you need to cut two identical parts on a band saw or a scroll saw, stack the two pieces of wood one on top of the other. Keep them from slipping out of alignment by bonding them temporarily with double-faced tape (such as carpet tape) placed between them.

66 Miter-making

A homemade miter for your table saw can assist you to cut perfect 45-degree angles every time. First fit two guide strips of hardwood into the tabletop grooves.

Next, glue a particle board base roughly 18×28 inches to the hardwood strips, making sure that the edge of the particleboard is squared with the table. Then cut a straight slot for the saw partway through the center of the board and mark 45-degree angles on both sides of the slot. Finally, attach 1×2 cleats along each angle line, with sandpaper affixed to the inside and outside edges of the cleats to prevent of the wood that is to be cut from slipping.

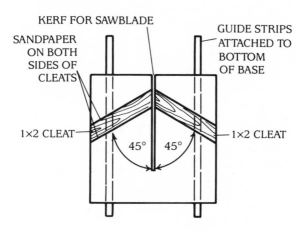

KERF FOR SAWBLADE

SANDPAPER ON BOTH SIDES OF CLEATS

GUIDE STRIPS ATTACHED TO BOTTOM OF BASE

1×2 CLEAT

1×2 CLEAT

45° 45°

67 Saw blade pocket

Circular saw blades present a tricky storage problem. If the teeth are badly nicked—which frequently happens when the blade is put away with other tools—the blade must be sharpened or replaced. Either process is expensive. To protect the teeth, insert the blade into the pocket of a school report cover and store the report cover in a drawer. Label the cover so you know what's inside without having to open it.

68 Table saw accessories

You can accumulate a sizable number of accessories for your power saw, including wrenches, saw fences, and miter guides. Instead of fumbling all over your workshop to find the accessory you need, make a storage board to hold all of them. Attach a section of perforated hardboard (peg board) to the side legs of your table saw stand and hang the accessories on hooks inserted in the holes.

69 Adjustable extension table

When you need an extension table for a table saw, use an old ironing board topped with a piece of hardboard, smooth side up. Simply adjust the legs of the ironing board to the same height as the table saw and place it alongside. When you're finished, you can easily fold up the extension and store it out of the way.

70 Two-way saw

Inevitably a hacksaw blade gets clogged as it cuts soft metal. To avoid this, put two blades side by side in the saw frame with the teeth facing in opposite directions. The cut will be twice as wide as a single blade, but the clogging problem will be eliminated. As one blade cuts, the debris accumulated in that stroke is dislodged by the debris produced by the other blade in the next stroke, in the other direction.

71 From ladder to saw horse

For many sawing jobs, a stepladder makes a convenient saw horse. Just lay the ladder on its side with its legs spread, and place the piece on which you want to work across the legs. Hold the piece steady with your hand and knee.

72 Stepladder latch

A stepladder should stay closed when you're carrying it or while it's being stored. To make sure that it does, install a standard window latch on the ladder. The two parts of the latch should be directly across from one another on each leg.

73 Stepladder clamp holder

Metal clamp holders—the type commonly used to grip mops and brooms by their handles—make excellent holders for small hand tools. Mount them on the end of the top step of your stepladder.

74 A guide for your router table

You can create a quick, easy, and sturdy router table guide with a C-clamp and a short length of hardwood or metal angle. Bolt one end of the guide to a corner of the router table. Use the C-clamp to secure the other end after swiveling it to the setting you want.

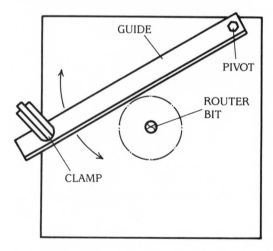

75 Portable vice

Occasionally it would be nice to have a small vise handy to work on a repair job away from your workbench. Create a portable vise by bolting a 3-inch vise to a scrap of wood roughly 2×12×15 inches. Fasten your portable vise to a firm, on-site support with two, easy-to-carry C-clamps.

76 Streamlined vise padding

Prevent the jaws of a vise from damaging the wood they are holding by covering the jaw faces with rubberized magnetic strips custom cut to fit. Magnetic strips are much more stable than wooden blocks and a lot less bulky.

77 Sawhorse tool saddle

Need a handy place to put your tools when you're working with sawhorses? Nail a square foot of ½-inch plywood to the top of one of the horses. It makes a good platform for keeping tools safely out of the way and yet within reach.

78 Soldering iron hanger

To keep a hot soldering iron from rolling around when you set it down, place it in a homemade metal rest. Bend the ends of a wire coat hanger downward to form a 2- or 3-inch leg at each end. Then bend the straight wire between them down slightly in the center to form a shallow V. Finally, bend the hook end downward to form a third leg. The resulting cradle will hold the iron safely with the tip in the V, elevated above the work surface, and the handle resting in the deep V where the wire is twisted together at the hook.

79 A light for tight places

When you're doing a small repair or maintenance job in a dark, cramped place, a heavy lantern or a rolling flashlight can be annoyingly inconvenient. Make a small, stable trouble light by plugging a night light into an extension cord. It lays flat, fits into tiny spaces, and offers a surprising amount of illumination.

80 A nail tie for hammer necks

Fit the upper part of your hammer handles with snug rubber bands. Whenever you have a nailing job that requires a limited number of nails, insert them under the band of the hammer you're using. That way, each nail is right at hand whenever you are ready for it.

81 Hammertop guard

When you're prying a nail out of wooden surface with the claws of a hammer, the top of the hammer can scratch or mark the surface. Prevent this from happening by making a hammertop guard out of a strip of rubber. Cut a round hole in one end of the strip for the head and a rectangular hole at the other end for the claws. Slip the strip over the hammerhead as shown to act as a tight-fitting protective shield.

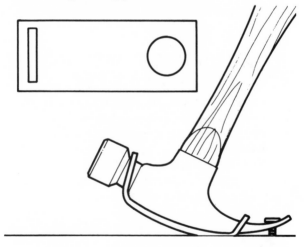

82 Chalk up your screwdriver

Like a pool cue, a screwdriver is less apt to slip if it is first chalked up. The next time you're faced with a stubborn or slippery screw head, try coating the tip of your screwdriver with standard blackboard chalk.

83 Turning a worn-down screw

If a screw head has been worn down or the slot has been badly damaged, a screwdriver may not be able to remove it. Instead of using a screwdriver in such a situation, try fitting a center punch into the screw slot. Put the point of the punch off-center to the right and at an angle and then tap the punch with a hammer to rotate the head counterclockwise until it is loose enough to work with a screwdriver.

84 Kinder, gentler pliers

Pliers can mark, dent, or abrade the surfaces they grip. If this is a concern, cushion each jaw of the pliers with a finger cut from an old rubber glove, or wrap each jaw with two or three layers of electrician's rubber tape. On really delicate surfaces, fold a sold cloth until it is several layers thick and use that to cushion the pliers.

85 Fitting a wrench that's too big

Sometimes it's necessary to make a box wrench—the kind with a hexagonal or other multisided hole in the end—fit more snugly around a nut. Try inserting a metal shim between the two. Or, if the gap is relatively big, you may be able to fill it with the tip of your screwdriver blade. If the gap is much bigger than that you need a different size wrench.

86 Give yourself a hand

Have you ever wished for another hand to hold small items that you're putting together or soldering? Make a convenient holder by wrapping a rubber band around the handles of a pair of long-nose pliers. It will pull the handles together, which will keep the jaws closed on the item you need held. Either that or get yourself an assistant!

87 No-pain panes

When you're cutting glass, these pointers will help you avoid fractures and uneven edges. First, use only a clean, sharp cutter. If the wheel is nicked or dull, get a new cutter; they are inexpensive. Second, brush turpentine or paint thinner along the line to be cut. This reduces surface friction and helps prevent skipping in the line cut into the surface. Third, press firmly as you draw the cutter along the cut line. Make one cut. Doing it a second time only increases the chances of getting poor edges or splits.

88 A riveting thought

When you're using rivets that have to be pounded down (peened) to make a permanent fastening (rather than self-peening pop rivets), be sure each rivet protrudes a bit more than its own diameter though the combined thickness of the pieces to be joined. Otherwise you won't have enough metal to form a good head when you hammer it.

89 Suction power

Suction cups can be attached to tools, chalk lines, and other accessories to hold them handy or in working position. A suction cup will remain stuck on a surface longer if it is rubbed over a slightly moistened bar of soap before being pressed in position. This will also help to avoid leaving a ring on the surface.

90 The tie that binds

Don't worry about accidentally pulling the plug out of an extension cord the next time you're working with a power tool. Beforehand, loop together the ends of the tool cord and the extension cord as if you were going to tie a knot. Then, instead of tightening the knot, plug in the cords together.

91 A tangled web

Whether it is a tangled 50 feet of extension cord or a snarled bunch of twine, the best way to straighten out a stringlike tangle is to pull outward all around the edges, making the mass looser and bigger. Some of the loops will untangle themselves, and it will then be much easier to find one end and unweave the remaining knots.

92 Clean by any means

To clean hand tools without leaving soap deposits or scratching cutting edges apply toothpaste with a damp rag. For tough deposits such as pastes and gums, try spray-on oven cleaner. Be sure to wear gloves.

93 Bright is dull

When does a knife blade, or a chisel edge, or saw teeth need sharpening? When it/they reflect light. A really sharp edge doesn't look bright because it is so thin. A dull edge is wider and thus more reflective.

94 Instant shear sharpening

When you need to sharpen shears or snips and you don't have the right sharpening tool at hand, grab a small piece of fine sandpaper and fold it in half with the rough side facing out. Then cut through the folded sandpaper three or four times with the dull shears or snips. You'll be surprised what a difference it makes.

95 Risk-free blade cleaning

When you clean a sharp knife or blade surface, don't jeopardize your fingers. Dip a cork into the cleaner and then rub it on the blade and the cutting edge.

96 Demagnetizing tools

Over time, pliers, screwdrivers, and other hand tools can become magnetized. This hinders their ability to function well around other metal surfaces. You can remove the magnetism from a tool with the help of an electric soldering gun. Simply pass the tool between the legs of the soldering tip two or three times while the gun is switched on.

97 Adjustable brush

If a repair job calls for a small, stiff brush and you don't have one, you can create a temporary substitute with a paintbrush and a strip of masking tape. Wrap the tape strip securely around the bristles near their tips. When the job is finished, remove the tape and the brush will return to its normal shape.

98 Metal-attracting dustpan

After sweeping the workshop, are you still likely to run across small nails or screws that fell out of the dustpan? Before you sweep again, glue a strip of flexible magnetic tape across the inside of the pan, near the rear. This will attract and hold small metal parts and debris, ensuring that you won't slip on them later or lose items that you want to retain.

99 Pantyhose filter

You can prolong the effectiveness of a workshop vacuum cleaner filter, plus keep it cleaner for a longer period of time, with a discarded pair of pantyhose. Cut off one leg of the pantyhose a bit long, tie one end, stretch the open end over the filter, and hold it in place with a large rubber band around the top. The resulting filter guard will have little effect on the vacuum's suction power. Save the other leg of the pantyhose for later use.

100 Broom handle brace

In time, the threaded end of a push broom handle is bound to loosen, making the brush twist and wobble whenever you sweep. Solve this problem with a pair of L-shaped brackets. Screw the brackets to the head of the broom on each side of the handle so it fits snugly between their upright legs. Then screw through the upright legs into the handle.

101 Oils well that ends well

To keep unvarnished or unpainted wooden handles on tools looking like new, wipe them down frequently with linseed oil. If a handle is a bit loose, try soaking it in the oil for a while. This will swell the wood and make for a tighter fit.

102 Chuck key safety measure

To reduce the odds of having an accident with a portable power tool, rig it so that it must be unplugged before you can use the chuck key. You can do this by taping the key securely near the plug end of the tool's electric cord.

103 Padlocked power tools

If you have small children, prevent them from ever being able to plug in a power tool by running a small padlock through the hole in one of the plug prongs. Only unplug the lock when you need to use the tool. Small padlocks are widely available at sundry and hardware stores. If you buy several at the same time, you'll have an ample supply of locks that use a common key—and an ample supply of extra keys to replace lost ones.

104 Safety plug

For safety's sake, it's a good idea to unplug a work-shop machine after you finish using it. To avoid having to search for the plug the next time you need it, install a screw eye opened partway, or a cup hook, next to the electrical outlet to hold the wire just below the plug.

105 Switch guard

To protect a switch from being accidentally turned on or off, place a guard over it. For full-size wall switches, bend a piece of sheet metal or a strip cut from a large can into a square U and drill holes so it can be held by the wall plate mounting screws. To protect fingers, cover the edges with tape or bend them over. For smaller switches, use a screen door or window sash handle. You can easily slip a finger under these to operate the switch.

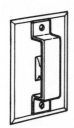 

106 White stripes for safety

Adults as well as children can injure themselves because they fail to realize that a power tool is actually running. If you paint white stripes on all the exposed moving parts of your power tools, you and everyone who comes near the tools will always be able to tell when they're in motion. The stripes should be roughly 3 inches apart and should be painted on every belt, chain, and saw blade, and they should run perpendicular to the line of motion.

107 Mask for protection

A major risk when you're working with power tools is getting sawdust in your eyes. Spare your eyes this risk by wearing shatterproof skindiving goggles whenever you're using a power tool. The goggles can also protect your eyes from drips when you're painting a ceiling.

3

MEASURING AND LEVELING

108 An edge on measuring

Customize your workspace and work equipment to provide built-in measuring instruments. Use nails to hold a yardstick horizontally along the front or side edge of the surface of your workbench. Simply lying there, it will come in handy for many workbench tasks. For the same reason, you may want to attach another yardstick to one of your sawhorses. A 6- or 12-inch plastic ruler glued flush to an outside edge of your toolbox saves time and effort when you need to know the exact lengths of nails, screws, and drill bits.

109 Yardstick marker

Your yardstick will be much handier on the job if it has a sliding marker that can indicate the most recent measurement. A rubber band twisted around the yardstick will work, but it's a bit awkward and you'll need to keep replacing it. Why not make a permanent band to fit around your yardstick from a ½-inch wide strip of mylar or acetate? Wrap it around the stick and secure the ends with tape. Although it needs to be slack enough for your fingers to slide it along, it should fit snugly enough to stay where you put it.

110 Precision drilling

Among the trickier aspects of drilling a hole is achieving the right depth. To solve this problem measure from the tip of a drill bit up along its shaft and wind a strip of masking tape at the depth you want. When you drill, stop when the bottom edge of the tape just reaches the surface of the piece you are working on.

111 Saw-stopper

The next time you have to make a shallow cut to a specific depth with a handsaw, create a depth gauge that will make sure you go no further. Use tape or C-clamps to attach wooden strips to either side of the saw at a distance above the teeth equal to the desired depth of the cut. When the strips touch the surface you are sawing, the job is finished.

112 Moonlighting depth gauge

An inexpensive gauge for measuring tire tread depth, available at hardware and auto supply stores, can also be used in home repair and maintenance jobs to measure shallow crevices. The typical gauge is marked in $\frac{1}{32}$-inch increments up to an inch: ideal for determining the depth of dado cuts, dowel pin holes, or wallboard cracks.

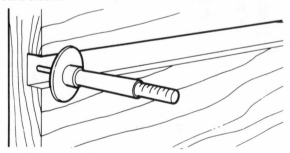

113 Winner by a yard

Want to spare yourself a lot of wasted time and effort when you're cutting wood on your sawhorse? Nail a yardstick on one side of the top horizontal beam and as close to the top edge as practical. You'll always know in an instant precisely where to make your cut.

114 White for good measure

Over time, the indented measurement lines in metal framing squares and yardsticks can become difficult to read. For a quick fix, rub a piece of chalk or white soap over the lines to increase their visibility. To heighten the contrast between the surface and the indented lines more permanently, first clean the surface with fine-grade steel wool. Clean dirt out of the lines with the point of a very slim brad. Then brush on a white oil-base paint, taking care to fill all the measurement marks. Lightly wipe the excess paint off the surface, leaving paint to dry in the indentations.

115 Sizing things up

Need to know the diameter of a nail or screw? Simply find the hole in a drill index that it fits into. A drill index is a metal holder for twist drill bits. It has a series of holes each marked with the diameter of the bit that fits into it.

116 Meaty display

Don't throw out those plastic foam trays used for packaging food products. Wipe them clean and record shop measurement tables and formulas on them with a felt-tip pen. Mounted on a wall with tacks or double-stick tape, the finished product is easy to read and more durable than paper.

117 Floor ruler

Your workshop floor is perhaps the most convenient place to measure long pieces of lumber. Make the task even easier by marking and labeling the length or width of the floor (whichever is more appropriate) in 6-inch intervals. You can paint lines across the floor itself or on the wall where it meets the floor. If you paint lines on the floor, you may want to varnish the lines after you've painted them to prevent them being erased or obscured by foot traffic. If your work area floor is covered with vinyl tiles, they are either 9 inches or 12 inches square. You can make measurements by counting tiles and multiplying by the appropriate figure.

118 Measuring bucket

A bucket gets used for mixing all sorts of chemical compounds, including cleaning solutions, insecticides, and plant foods. Make the mixing task easier by marking the inside of the bucket to indicate different volumes, such as a pint, a quart, two quarts, a gallon, two gallons. Use a permanent felt-tip marker.

119 A ruler of thumbs

By investing just a few minutes of time, you can make sure that you always have a reasonably accurate measuring device around. Simply measure different spans on your body and memorize those calculations. Among the most useful measurements are:

- the distance between different finger or thumb joints (experiment and you can probably establish a 1-inch length);
- the spread of your splayed hand, from the tip of your thumb to the tip of your little finger;
- the length of your outstretched arm from the tip of your longest finger to your armpit;
- the length of your foot.

120 Measure by the dollar

When you want to measure something at home or in the hardware store and you don't have a tape measure or ruler handy, try using a dollar bill. It's 6$\frac{1}{8}$ inches long, 3$\frac{1}{16}$ inches when folded in half, and almost exactly 1$\frac{1}{2}$ inches when folded in quarters. Its full width is 2$\frac{5}{8}$ inches, or fractionally more than 1$\frac{1}{4}$ inches when folded in half lengthwise. Ignoring minor frac-

tions, this gives you a ruler to measure 6, 3, 2½ ,
1½ , and 1¼ inches almost always in your pocket.

121 A hammer for good measure

Most often you need two hands for hammering in
nails: One to hold the hammer and the other to hold
the nail. This makes it awkward when you also need
to measure where to put the nails, especially if you're
high up on a ladder. To make such measuring tasks
much easier, wrap thin strips of tape around the handle of the hammer to mark intervals of 3 inches, 9
inches, 12 inches, and (if possible) 15 inches from the
top of the hammer head. Or mark the intervals with a
permanent marker or paint.

122 Post hole probe

You don't have to stop digging a post hole in order to
measure your progress. Before you start, mark one
handle of the post-hole digger or your shovel with a
strip of paint at a point 1 foot from the tip of the digger scoops or the shovel blade and at 6-inch intervals
after that. This way, you'll never dig deeper than you
need to.

123 Measuring around corners

A flexible retractable ruler does an excellent job of
measuring around corners. It can also fit easily into
angular cracks and crevices, which, in many cases,
will serve to hold the ruler in place while you work.

124 Measurement prompt

Don't forget measurements you need in the course of
working on a repair or maintenance project. Put a
piece of masking tape on your measuring stick or the
case of your retractable tape and write those measurements on the masking tape. When you're through

with the project, peel the tape off and either throw it away or save it for future reference.

125 Copying an irregular line

The next time you need to reproduce an irregular line—for example, to cut a panel or flooring to go around molding or to fit snugly against a stone wall—use a drawing compass as a scribing tool. Butt the piece to be marked up against the greatest projection of the irregular surface. Move the compass so its point traces over the irregularities; the marking leg will trace a matching line on the surface to be cut.

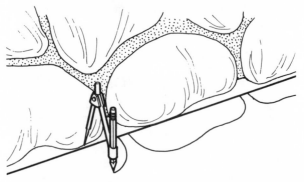

126 Lining up holes

Need to line up screw or plug holes for a shelving project so that the shelves will wind up being perfectly level? A piece of pegboard can be helpful, as long as it's big enough. Just hang it on a couple of nails over the surface that you want to drill into, making sure that its horizontal rows are perfectly level, and use appropriately located holes to mark the points where you need to drill.

127 Plumb bob mount

A small rubber suction cup with an attached eye bolt makes a great hanger for the string of a plumb bob.

The suction cup will adhere to almost any surface without leaving a mark. It will even stick to a ceiling.

128 Keep your bob from bobbing

When you're working outdoors with a plumb bob, the wind can keep the plumb bob from remaining in a steady up and down position for vertical alignments. Solve this problem by placing a bucket of water under the plumb bob the weight itself hangs in the water. Because of the diameter of the bucket, the object you're aligning (for example, a post) cannot be aligned directly against the plumb bob cord. But when the distance between the object and the cord is the same at the top and near the bottom, it is aligned vertically with the cord.

129 Leveling a level

Want to check that a level is really accurate? Set it on a table or the floor, mark its location with a pencil, and record the bubble positions in relation to the index marks in the vial. Then rotate the level 180 degrees end-for-end, set it on the location marks, and record those bubble readings. Next, turn the level over so that it rests on its other side. Make the same two sets of readings, using the same location marks. All four sets of bubble readings should be the same. If not, use the level's adjusting screws to adjust the vial until all readings match, or look for another level.

130 Getting it straight

Posts for decks or fences must be plumb and perpendicular or the finished structure will eventually sag. This requires repeated checking during setting to make sure posts haven't moved. To minimize the hassle, use Velcro strips to strap your level to each post as you work on it. For greater support, glue two small patches of Velcro close to the ends of the level to serve as "hooks" for the Velcro loops securing the level to the post. One note of caution: Don't hammer on a post with a level strapped to it.

131 Level and holding

A metal level tends to slip when it's held against a smooth wall. Give it some gripping power by gluing small strips of sandpaper along the sides. If you use rubber cement, the sections can be easily removed.

132 Off-level reading

To modify your level to align something at a certain pitch, move the level to the pitch or slope you want. Then mark the off-center bubble position by putting a strip of tape on the bubble window at each end of the bubble. This is more accurate than trying to mark the window with a crayon or grease pencil. To get the same pitch elsewhere, simply move the level until the bubble is centered between the two tapes. When you're finished, remove the tape.

133 Substitute level

When you need to mark a level line across a vertical surface such as a wall and you don't have a level, try this trick instead. Lay a ¾-inch thick board with a straight edge flat across the surface. Then place a marble on the top edges of the board, midway along the length. When the board is level, the marble won't roll one way or the other.

134 Light test for straightness

To check the straightness of a short board or other piece of material, hold the edge or surface against a straightedge, such as the arm of a carpenter's square or the edge of a level. If the board rocks, it bows downward between the ends. The point at which it rocks is the point of maximum bowing. If it does not rock, look at the line between the piece and the straightedge against a strong light. If light shines through, the piece bows upward.

135 True measure of lumber

Actual lumber sizes differ somewhat from the nominal sizes the industry uses to designate lumber. The nominal size refers to the nearest whole-inch measurement when a piece is rough-cut from a log in a mill. The piece then goes through a planer that smooths all four surfaces, removing some wood in the process. As a result, the finished size that you purchase is smaller than its designation. A board sold as 2×6 board in reality measures 1½ x 5½ inches. Narrower boards are also ½ inch less in each declared dimension with one exception: Lumber designated as 1 inch thick is, in fact, ¾ inch thick. For boards declared to be 8 inches wide or greater, the actual width is ¾ inch less.

136 Inches and pennies

Confused by nail designations such as "4-penny," "8-penny," and so on (commonly abbreviated 4d, 8d, etc.)? To determine the penny size of a particular nail length, the following method works for lengths up to 3 inches (10d). Take the length of nail you need, subtract ½ inch, and multiply by 4. For example, if you need a 2½-inch nail, subtract ½ inch, which leaves 2. Multiply by 4. What you need is an 8-penny nail.

137 Pennies and inches

Need to know what a penny size means in terms of nail length? Divide the penny size by 4 and add ½ inch to get the length in inches. For example, 6d divided by 4 equals 1½ plus ½ equals 2 inches. The method works for nails up to 10d (3 inches).

138 Converting to and from metric

Use the following techniques to convert linear measurements to and from the metric system; they are accurate to within ± 0.09%.

1. There are 25.4 millimeters per inch. To convert millimeters to inches, divide by 25 and subtract ¼ inch for every 15 inches in the converted answer. To convert from inches to millimeters, add ¼ inch for every 15 inches in the dimension, then multiply by 25.

2. There are 39⅜ (39.37) inches per meter. To convert meters to inches, multiply by 40 and subtract 2 inches for every 3 meters in the original dimension. To convert inches to meters, add ¼ inch for every 36 inches in the original dimension, then divide by 40.

139 Quickest way to the middle

Need to find the middle of a board quickly? Avoid trying to divide odd numbers and difficult fractions such as 9¹³⁄₁₆ inches in half. Simply lay a ruler diagonally across the board so that an even-numbered inch mark is at each edge. The inch mark halfway between them points to the exact center of the board. Don't have a ruler? Fold a sheet of paper in half to mark its center, unfold it, and lay it across the board with the corners of one long side at opposite sides of the board. The crease in the middle indicates the center of the board.

140 Hitting dead center

The next time you need to locate the exact center of a circular object, use this technique: Lay a right-angled corner (for example, the corner of a piece of paper or a carpenter's square) inside the circle so that the point of the corner touches the circumference. Then mark the circumference where each side of the angle crosses it. Draw a line between these two points—that is a diameter of the circle. Repeat this process with the corner of the right angle touching another point of the circumference. Where the two diameters cross is the exact center of the circle.

141 How far away?

When you need to know the distance to an inaccessible object, geometry can do the job without any complex figuring. All you need is a measuring tape and the ability to make lines at right angles—for example, by sighting along the legs of a carpenter's square. The diagram shows the method:

1. To determine the distance from A to the inaccessible X, drive a stake at A. Then establish line A–C at right angles to a line from A to X.

2. Measure a good distance along this new line and drive a stake at C. Also drive a stake at B, exactly halfway between A and C.

3. Now establish a right-angle line from C running in the direction of D. Move along this line until you reach the point where X lines up with B as you sight across B with one eye. Drive a stake at this point, D.

4. Measure the distance C–D; the distance A–X will be the same.

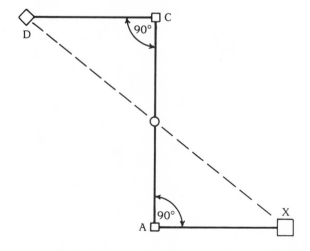

142 How high is up?

An easy way to measure the approximate height of a tall object, such as a flagpole, is to use shadows. On a sunny day, measure the length of the shadow the pole casts on the ground, from the base outward. Drive a stick vertically into the ground nearby. Measure its height and the length of its shadow. The pole height and the stick height will be in the same ratio as their two shadows. For example, if the pole shadow is eight times longer than the stick shadow, its height is eight times the stick height. (If you want to use pencil and paper, or a calculator, divide the pole shadow length by the stick shadow length, then multiply by the stick height—just be sure all measurements are in the same units, feet or inches, metrics or whatever. The result is the height of the pole.)

143 Graphic help

Keep a supply of graph paper on hand for making notes and correctly proportioned and scaled sketches regarding repair and maintenance projects. Graph paper drawings are especially helpful when you go shopping in hardware, lumber, and plumbing supply stores, so be sure to take them with you.

144 Calculating areas

To determine the area of a square or rectangle, multiply the width times the length. To determine the area of a circle, use the formula 3.14 (pi) × the radius squared. To determine the area of an irregular shape, draw the shape on graph paper. Then count the whole squares and add your estimate of the number of whole squares that could be made by putting together the partial squares. The actual area depends on whether each square in your drawing represents 1 inch, 1 foot, 1 yard, or some other unit.

145 Area of tiled floor or ceiling

Standard floor and ceiling tiles come in 9-inch or 12-inch squares. A quick way to get the square footage of a ceiling or floor covered with standard tiles is first to ascertain the tile size. Then count the number of tiles along the length and width of the room. With 12-inch tiles the square footage of the ceiling is equal to the number of tiles in the length multiplied by the number in the width.

With 9-inch tiles, you can multiply the number of tiles each way by 9, multiply the two totals together, and then divide by 144 (the number of square inches in a square foot). Or you can multiply the number of tiles together, as with 12-inch tiles, and take 56.5 percent of the answer (multiply by 0.565).

For example, with 12-inch tiles an area 10 tiles by 8 tiles = 80 square feet. With 9-inch tiles, it equals (10×9)×(8×9) = 90×72 = 6480, divided by 144 = 45 square feet. Or, 80×0.565 = 45.2 square feet.

146 How many rolls of wallcovering?

Figuring out how many rolls of wallcovering to buy for the area you want to cover is a complicated task. Most wallcovering rolls contain 36 square feet, meaning that the actual length of the roll varies according to its width. However, wallcovering is usually sold in "double roll" form, that is, the roll you purchase is the same width but twice the length of a single roll. Your best bet is to calculate your needs based on a formula of 30 square feet per roll/60 square feet per double roll because there is bound to be some waste.

147 A good mix

For outdoor concrete slabs for patios, sidewalks, driveways, and such, a good mix is 1 part cement, 2.5 parts sand, and 3.5 parts large aggregate (gravel). The aggregate should be a mixture of stone sizes, with the largest no more than about one-fourth the thickness of the slab to be poured. For example, for a 6-inch-thick slab, the aggregate should have stones 1½ inches in diameter and smaller.

148 How much concrete?

To determine how many cubic feet or cubic yards of concrete you need for a slab, figure the total area to be covered in square feet. Then, in the table below look under the column for the thickness of the slab you want to pour. Use the cubic feet data to work out the materials needed to mix the concrete yourself; use the cubic yard data to order ready-mixed concrete (minimum order usually 1 cu. yd.). Add or multiply figures to get the quantities for other sizes. For example, for a 5-inch slab, add the appropriate quantities given for 2- and 3-inch slabs. For a 45-square-foot slab of a given thickness, multiply the amount for a 15-foot slab by 3.

Slab Area (sq. ft.)		Quantity of Concrete for Slab Thickness of			
		2"	3"	4"	6"
15	cu. ft.	2.5	3.75	5.0	7.5
	cu. yd.	0.1	0.15	0.2	0.3
20	cu. ft.	3.3	5.0	6.7	10.0
	cu. yd.	0.1	0.2	0.3	0.4
50	cu. ft.	8.3	12.5	16.7	25.0
	cu. yd.	0.3	0.5	0.6	0.9
75	cu. ft.	12.5	18.75	25.0	37.5
	cu. yd.	0.5	0.7	0.9	1.4
100	cu. ft.	16.7	25.0	33.3	50.0
	cu. yd.	0.6	0.9	1.2	1.9
150	cu. ft.	25.0	37.5	50.0	75.0
	cu. yd.	0.9	1.4	1.9	2.8
200	cu. ft.	33.3	50.0	66.7	100.0
	cu. yd.	1.2	1.9	2.5	3.7

149 Gauging oil drum volume

Most oil tanks consist of 55-gallon drums. To determine the amount of oil left in a vertical drum, dip a stick marked in inches to the bottom of the drum. Every 2⅞ inches of oil on the stick equals five gallons. To determine the amount of oil left in a *horizontal* drum, use this table:

Inches	Gallons	Inches	Gallons
16	44	8	18
15	41	7	15
14	38	6	12
13	35	5	9
12	31	4	7
11	28	3	4
10	25	2	2
9	22	1	1

150 Propane depth

To find out how much liquid propane is left in a tank, wipe a streak down the outside of the tank, from top to bottom, with a wet sponge. The moisture will evaporate from the upper, empty portion of the tank faster than from the lower portion that contains the liquified gas. You can easily see whether the tank is about ⅔, ½, or ⅓ full.

151 Check gas line joints

To check propane or natural gas line joints and fittings, paint them with liquid laundry/dish detergent slightly thinned with water. If any gas is escaping, it will create bubbles in the detergent coating.

152 One tape for the road

The next time you wear out a tape measure, cut off a 4-inch section with clear markings and keep it in your wallet. You'll be surprised how handy it will be to check the exact sizes of hardware items when you're shopping.

153 Keeping a level hedge

It's very difficult to trim a hedge so that the top is level along the entire length. You can achieve this goal by driving temporary poles into the ground at the beginning and end of the hedge and wherever the hedge turns or curves. Run a string from pole to pole that is always exactly level at the height you want. Follow this guide as you trim and you'll wind up with a uniformly level hedge.

154 A straight paneling job

If you want to make sure that the paneling you're installing is uniformly vertical, make sure to get the first panel right, so that you can line up the others accordingly. First align this panel against the corner and hold it there with one nail hammered part way into the top. Then use a level to determine if the outside edge is truly vertical. If not, scribe the edge in the corner and trim it as required to match the adjoining wall. When it hangs vertically, nail the panel permanently in place.

4

PAINTING, WALLPAPERING, AND REFINISHING

155 Grease and oil busters

Grease and oil spots must be removed from all surfaces that you paint or varnish. Usually, these spots are fairly small, making alcohol prep pads ideal for dissolving them and wiping them away. Prep pads are first-aid items—small cotton squares saturated with alcohol that are individually foil-packaged. They are sold in drugstores and pharmacies.

156 Finishing removal options

Stripping wood with a highly toxic chemical remover is a messy and unpleasant job. First, try mixing a solution of equal parts of boiled linseed oil, white vinegar, and turpentine or mineral spirits and rubbing it into the wood with fine-grade steel wool.

157 Keep stripper in place

Liquid paint stripper has a bad habit of dripping off woodwork and other vertical wood surfaces and, therefore, not doing its job as quickly or as thoroughly as it should. Dribbling sawdust over the stripper remedies this. It will help the stripper adhere to the wood. Even better than sawdust is whiting, sold in paint supply stores. It doesn't absorb as much stripper into its body, leaving more to work on the surface.

158 Homemade stripper

Make your own stripper for removing paint from hardware. Stir a pound of wood ashes in four gallons of water. This will release caustic sodium and potassium hydroxides. Then, wearing heavy rubber gloves, place the hardware gently in the solution. Let it soak it overnight. The next day, again wearing heavy rubber gloves, remove the hardware and scrub it thoroughly with a toothbrush.

159 Removing paint from hardware

To clean exterior door and window hardware that's covered with old paint, dirt, or pollutants place the pieces in a pan filled with cold water and roughly 4 tablespoons of baking soda per quart. Set the pan over low heat on a stove burner and keep the solution simmering for 20 minutes. Then remove the hardware and scrub off all remaining particles with steel wool. Repeat the procedure for hard-to-remove spots.

160 Gleaming brass

To clean and polish unlacquered brass, wipe it with a damp cloth dipped in Worcestershire sauce, and then wipe clean with another soft damp cloth. If lacquer is cracked or peeling, remove it completely with lacquer thinner before cleaning the piece.

161 Paint-free scraper

When you're stripping paint with a heat gun, some of the hot paint will inevitably stick to the scraper and find its way back on the wall again. Keep this from happening by coating the scraper with no-stick cooking spray before you begin stripping.

162 Steel wool and wood

To put an ultrasmooth surface on wood that you want to refinish, use the finest grade of steel wool you can buy instead of sandpaper for the final preparatory sanding. Then remove any minute metal slivers from the wood before refinishing it by slowly running a magnet over the entire surface.

163 Advice on door painting

The next time you're about to repaint a door, first sand the edges well. Otherwise the added layer of paint may make the door stick in the frame after the paint dries.

164 Out, moldy spot!

Siding or roofing on a shady, moist end of a house may develop patches of mold, mildew, or other surface growths. To get rid of this problem, spray each spot with a diluted solution of household bleach, using a plastic bottle pump spray for small areas, or a garden sprayer for large areas. Let the bleach solution sit for 30 to 60 minutes, then wash it away with a hose.

165 Short-term brush storage

Hold onto moistened-towelette containers. Many have cover openings that provide an excellent grip for brush handles. When you want to take a short break from painting, varnishing, staining, or enameling, insert the brush handle up through the slits in the cover from underneath so that the brush bristles hang free when you put the cover back on. Sealed off from outside air, the brush will stay moist for a couple of hours. You can also fill the container with solvent or water, according to the kind of paint you are using, to clean the bristles between applications or to keep them fresher for a longer period of time.

166 Temporary brush block

Here's a tip for making your paintbrush easier to pick up and set down while you're painting. Before you begin, tape a scrap of wood 1×1 or a similar block across the ferrule—(the part of the handle that holds the bristles). Then, you can rest the brush on this block when you want to put it down. The bristles will stick up into the air, and paint won't get on anything it shouldn't.

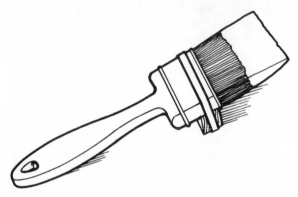

167 Smoother spray-painting

For a good spray-painted finish, you must keep the paint gun approximately the same distance from the surface throughout the spraying. Make this challenge easier by taping a stick to the spray gun that's an inch short of the desired working distance from the surface. While you're spraying, hold the spray gun so that this stick remains about an inch away from the surface at all times.

168 No-clog paint spraying

Paint sprayer nozzles are notorious for clogging easily between paint jobs. Don't give them a chance. After spray painting, remove the nozzles and keep them in a sealed jar filled with paint thinner.

169 Spray booth

Need to spray-paint a small item? Set it inside a cardboard box laid on its side. This will serve as a "spray booth" to keep the paint from spreading where you don't want it.

170 Unclogging spray cans

Frustrated by having to throw away partially used cans of spray paint just because the nozzle mechanism is clogged with dry paint? The next time you finish spray painting, turn the can completely upside down and spray until it's clear. The nozzle mechanism will then be free of paint and ready to work again.

171 Portable paint shield

One of the easiest and most effective ways to paint a smooth edge is to use a hand-held steel float, also known as a cement finishing trowel, as a masking device. Just move the float along as you paint. Afterwards, paint can be cleaned off the float's metal surface with very little trouble. Another shield is a scrap of metal or plastic slat from a venetian blind.

172 Touch-up brush

For touching up a paint job, use a small piece of foam sponge—about ¾ inch by 2 inches—doubled over and clamped in a spring-type clothespin. When you're finished, there's no unwanted clean-up: just throw away the piece of sponge and save the clothespin for the next touch-up job.

173 Painting an uneven floor

Wooden floors, especially on porches or on additions over a crawl space, can be uneven and therefore difficult to paint. To paint an uneven floor, use an acoustic tile roller, available at most paint and hardware stores. It's made of foam rubber that is cut every ¼ inch to allow the roller surface to conform with significant surface irregularities. This handy piece of equipment helps guarantee an even layer of paint.

174 Extension brush

To paint behind heavy objects that you can't or don't want to move—like a radiator, a piano, or a refrigerator—staple a section of plastic sponge onto the end of a yardstick or a thin wooden lath. The sponge can hold paint without dripping and will coat the surface behind the object with a nice smooth finish.

175 Ladder basket

To hold paint cans, brushes, or other items while working on a stepladder, use a basket mounted on the ladder's shelf. A plastic basket commonly known as a "household basket" works best. Just run an elastic shock cord under the ladder shelf and hook it into the openings in the sides of the basket.

176 Extension ladder extension

Metal extension ladders often have hollow rungs. When you're painting on an extension ladder, push a piece of a broom handle or a plastic water pipe through a waist-high rung and use it to hold your paint can. Be sure that this piece extends for about a foot from either side of the ladder and that the end holding the paint can has a notch in which to rest the handle.

177 When paint's running short

Any time that you see you're running low on paint as you're painting the walls of a room, make every effort to paint only the walls that you can cover completely with the current supply. A new can of paint—custom-mixed or not—is likely to be slightly different in shade; therefore, it's a good idea to avoid using paint from two different cans on the same wall.

178 Spring or fall to paint

The best seasons to paint outdoors are spring and fall. The weather is moderate (not too hot on you or the paint) and leaf-bearing plants and trees are bare, which means they're less likely to bother—or be bothered by—the paint.

179 Paint and weathering

Outside walls weather differently according to the direction they face. A south-facing wall is apt to receive approximately twice as much weathering from the sun as a north wall, and so it may have to be painted twice as often. Another variable is the prevailing direction of wind and rain: A wall exposed to the brunt of the wind and rain may also have to be painted more often. Consider these factors when planning the best long-range house-repainting strategy.

180 Best order of outdoor painting

Schedule the times at which you will paint different parts of the house according to where the sun will be. If you can avoid it, do not paint in direct sunlight. The glare from a light color can be very fatiguing. The higher temperature will increase the chances of runs. And blisters are more likely to form because the surface of the paint layer will dry faster than the underlying body, which leaves solvent trapped below the skin, and also leaves the paint softer and more susceptible to damage for a longer time. Don't paint on windy days, or painted surfaces may get pitted before they've dried. Try to paint windows and doors very early in the day so that they are dry to the touch by late afternoon.

181 Not all at once

Painting the exterior of a house often gets put off because it's such a big job—and the bigger the house, the longer the job tends to get delayed. But why be overwhelmed? There's no law that you must do it all at once. In Sweden and other northern countries where exterior finishes encounter severe weather conditions, it is common to do one side of the house each year. That keeps the work easily manageable while getting to all parts of the exterior frequently enough to avoid deterioration.

182 Stairway painting

When you're painting stairs, leave some room to walk up and down the stairway while the paint is drying. There are two ways to do this. Either paint half the width of each tread first and let them dry before painting the other half, or paint every other tread first and let those dry before painting the rest.

183 How much paint?

Use the chart below to determine how much paint to buy for the job you're doing. Remember that a second coat, on the average, requires only about ⅔ as much paint as a first coat.

Paint Coverage

First Coat	Surface Coverage (per gal)
Exterior rough or porous surface	90–110 sq. ft.
Exterior smooth surface	375–425 sq. ft.
Interior rough or porous surface	120–190 sq. ft.
Interior smooth surface	420–490 sq. ft.

184 Another paint estimate

Here's another way to find out how much paint you will need for the outside of a house. Figure the total number of square feet to be covered and subtract the window and door areas. Then add 10 percent for any area covered by lap siding, 20 percent for any area with a rough or porous surface, and 30 percent for any area covered with corrugated material. If you are putting a first coat on concrete or cinder blocks, add 50 percent for that area. Multiply your final figure by the number of coats of paint you will apply. Divide that total by the manufacturer's square-feet-per gallon coverage figure (usually listed on the instruction label). This will provide you with the minimum number of gallons required.

185 Calculating radiator area

Want to know how much paint to buy to cover all the ins and outs of your steam radiator? First determine the square footage of the front of the radiator by multiplying the length times the height. Then multiply this figure by seven.

186 Clean edge when painting

If you want an especially clean edge because you're painting a stripe along a wall, try this technique. Using a straightedge, draw a straight line on the wall with the back edge of a utility knife, creating a small indentation in the wall along the line you'll want the stripe to follow. If you paint carefully up to this line, the paint will fill into the slight indentation and give you the clean line you need.

187 Unmasking tape

When you're through painting, remove masking tape from the surfaces as soon as the paint has set. Otherwise the adhesive will bond to the surface and make the tape more difficult to remove cleanly. It's especially important not to let the tape bake in direct sunlight. If you're worried about the tape coming off cleanly, blow hot air from a hair dryer over each piece of tape before attempting to remove it. This will soften the adhesive so that the entire piece will come off easily, without disturbing the new paint.

188 A bold stroke with rollers

When you're using a paint roller, the job goes faster and produces a better looking paint job if you begin by getting a lot of paint on the surface and then focus on smoothing it out. To accomplish this, first paint a large "M" on the surface and then another large "M" on top of it at a right angle. Next, go back and spread the paint evenly.

189 Invisible touch-ups

It's difficult to do touch-up painting without leaving brush marks, especially on metal surfaces. Use cotton swabs instead of a brush. They fit into difficult places, are quite inexpensive, and can be thrown out when the job is finished.

190 Getting rid of paint job flaws

Don't pick bristles, dust motes, or runs out of a painted surface once it's started to form a skin. Wait until the paint dries, then rub down the surface with a moistened towelette. The result will look much neater.

191 Mini-stilts for furniture

When you're painting chairs, tables, or other furniture don't risk having the freshly painted legs stick to the paper or tarp underneath. Before you begin, drive a small nail into each leg that will hold it above the paper or tarp during painting and drying. Later, the nails can easily be removed.

192 "Both-side" coating

It is tiresome to wait for one side of a door or panel to dry before turning it over to paint, varnish, or stain the other side. If there is an overhead beam you can hang the door from, try this technique for working on one side right after the other. At one end above the door position, run a rope across the top of the beam, or fasten it at two points as shown. Cross the ends of the rope as they come down to form an X and tie them to nails that protrude 2 or 3 inches from the door end. Do exactly the same at the other end of the door. Adjust the rope lengths so the door hangs at a convenient working height. After finishing the first side, use the nails at one end as handles to turn the door over, uncrossing the Xs in the ropes and leaving the other side facing upward. With a big or heavy door you may want a helper at the other end to turn it over.

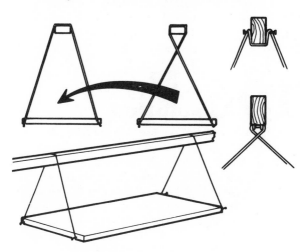

193 Foil-safe painting

Before painting an indoor room, use aluminum foil to cover items that are difficult to protect with a plastic sheeting or newspapers. Such items include plumbing fixtures, door knobs, telephone receivers, and wall lamps. The aluminum foil molds tightly to awkward shapes and is easy to remove and replace.

194 Bag that paint-covered hand!

Whenever you're painting, keep a couple of plastic sandwich bags handy. That way, if you need to open a door or answer the telephone, you can slip your hand in a bag and use it like a glove, without worrying about getting paint on the doorknob or the telephone.

195 On-the-ball painting

Want to keep paint from dripping down the brush onto your hand while you're painting? Slit the top and bottom of a small rubber ball (such as a racquetball) and insert the brush handle through the two slits. Hold the handle just below the ball while you're painting. This way, any paint that drips from the bristles will fall onto the ball, where it will spread on the surface and dry without reaching your hand.

196 A gripping solution

Before painting an outdoor porch floor, deck, or stairs, whether made of wood or masonry, mix fine white sand into the paint: about one part sand to four parts paint. This will keep the painted surface from becoming slippery when it gets wet with water. As you paint with this mixture, be sure to stir the paint frequently to keep the sand suspended and evenly dispersed.

197 Painting inside downspouts

Most rust problems in downspouts progress from the inside out. Here's a trick for giving the inside of a downspout a protective coat of paint. First, drop a string with a weight on it all the way through the downspout. Next, at the longer end tie the string to a sponge that is small enough to compress inside the downspout and be pulled through it, but big enough to fill the downspout all the way around. Then, with the sponge situated just inside the bottom of the downspout, pour a quantity of paint in from the top and give it time to flow to the bottom, where it will be stopped by the sponge. Finally, pull the string so that the sponge travels slowly up the downspout, spreading the paint against the wall of the downspout as it goes. After this coat is dry, repeat the process to make sure that the interior of the downspout is completely covered with paint.

198 Vitamin C for fumes

After exposure to fumes from paint, finishing solutions, or thinners, increase your intake of vitamin C, which acts as an antitoxicant. Although its precise protective value in any given situation of this nature is difficult to specify, scientific research has established that it can reduce or eliminate adverse effects from chemical fumes. Take a vitamin C pill or consume a food product rich in vitamin C, such as a piece of citrus fruit or a glass of citrus juice.

199 Preservative safety

Although it looks like a varnish and is applied like paint, wood preservative is neither. It's a pesticide that works by repelling animals and plants. When using and storing it, take extra precautions for your own safety and the safety of others. Wear gloves, avoid breathing the fumes, and keep the preservative separate from paints, cleaners, and refinishing solutions. Store it tightly sealed, in the garage or other outbuilding rather than in the basement or utility room.

200 Interior color tricks

When choosing interior paint colors, consider the following. A light color makes a room look larger, cooler, and drier. A dark color, on the other hand, makes a room look smaller, warmer, and cozier. A ceiling appears higher when it's painted a lighter color than the walls. A darker color makes a ceiling appear lower, plus it masks flaws in the surface better. If one side of a narrow hallway is painted a slightly darker shade of the color on the opposite side, the hallway as a whole will appear wider than it really is.

201 Exterior color tricks

When choosing exterior paint colors, consider the following. Emphasizing vertical elements will make a low, squat house look better proportioned. This involves painting items like doors, shutters, and corner trim in a color that offers either a light or dark contrast to the siding color. Conversely, emphasizing horizontal elements will make a tall, narrow house look better proportioned. This involves painting items like windowsills, flower boxes, foundations, fascia boards, and roofline gutters in a color that offers either a light or dark contrast to the siding color.

202 Disappearing primer

Primer paint is generally white, and, therefore, may show through a single coat of a dark color painted on top of it. To alleviate this problem, add a tube of tint to the primer so that it will be closer in color to the desired finish color.

203 No drippy paint cans

You can make a good striker—a device to scrape excess paint off a brush—out of an old paint can lid. Cut the lid in half and bend down the cut edge slightly so it isn't sharp. This half-lid will fit securely onto a paint can with the same size lid. Simply pull the brush across its edge to get rid of excess paint. An alternative is to stretch one or more pieces of masking tape over the open top of the can. Either striker can also be used as a brush rest while you are painting.

204 Perforated paint can rim

When you first remove a paint can lid, use a hammer and nail to punch four or five holes in the bottom of the groove around the inside the rim of the can. This will allow paint that gets into the rim to drain back into the can, preventing accidental squirts when you put the lid back on.

205 Box that paint

To avoid variations in color when a job will take two or more cans of paint, box their contents. Professionals call it boxing the paint. Open all the cans. Pour half the contents of one can into an extra container. Pour part of the second and third cans into the first one, and another part into the extra container. Then pour back and forth between all the containers several times to insure a uniform blend. Use the same general procedure with a greater number of cans. Finally, divide the blended paint among the original containers and seal them tightly until ready to be used.

206 Paint lump management

Does the old paint you want to use contain lumps? Don't try to break them up or you'll wind up brushing small pieces onto the surface you're painting. Strain the lumpy paint through window screening into another container. Let the accumulated lumps rest on the screen for about ten minutes so that as much paint can drain from them as possible, then discard them.

207 Blotter test for color

When you want to see what a paint color will look like when it's dry, stroke it with a brush across a clean white blotter. The blotter will quickly absorb the oils or other vehicle, leaving the paint the same color it will have when it dries on a wall.

208 On-the-spot record

Mark all paint or wallcovering information on the back of a switch plate in a room. You may also want to dab some of the paint itself here. This will give you a permanent in-place record for future reference, and a handy reminder to carry with you when you need to purchase matching supplies. If you do take the switch plate away, however, be sure to replace it temporarily with another one, for safety.

209 Combination prier-stirrer

Be prepared the next time you have to open a can of fresh paint. Make a combination tool out of a paint stirrer and a metal mending plate. Bolt the plate to the end of the stirrer handle, so that just an inch or so of the plate extends beyond the handle. This will give the plate enough leverage to pry the lid off of a paint can. Then turn the device around and use the stirring end to mix the paint.

210 Two-can painting for safety

It's always better to work from a paint can that is half full than from a paint can that is completely full. With a half full can, there's less chance of spills and drips. When you open a fresh can of paint, pour half of it into a second can. Then pour it back and forth between the two cans to make sure there's an equal mix of pigment and liquid in each can. Use the second can to hold the working supply while you're painting; keep the original can sealed until you need more paint.

211 Super-stirring

Want to mix paint faster and more effectively? Drill several holes down the length of your stirring paddle. Every stroke you make with this customized paddle will agitate the paint much more extensively. Use 1/4-inch holes in a metal stirrer, but 3/8-inch holes in a wood stirrer because of its greater thickness.

212 Good brush-dipping strategy

To cut down the risk of drips from your paintbrush and your paint can, never load more than half the length of the bristles with paint. When pulling the brush out, tap it gently against the inside of the can a couple of times but don't wipe it on the edge.

213 Milk carton mixer

Hold on to empty half-gallon milk cartons when you know a paint job is coming up. With the top cut off and washed clean, they make wonderful mixing containers. The paint doesn't stick to the plastic surface, and the square corners allow for easy pouring. The cartons can also be used as small, portable paint containers while you're painting.

214 Paint can depth marker

When you've finished a painting job, dunk a long, straight stick slowly into the paint, keeping it vertical. Then pull it out and stand it up for the paint to dry. In addition to showing you the depth of paint in the can, the stick can function as a convenient color reference. If you want to shop for the same color or a complementary color, or if you want to check that color against another color in the house, all you have to do is take the stick with you. Otherwise, keep it fastened to the paint can with tape, string, or a rubber band.

215 Spill-proof paint tray

To keep a paint can from accidentally tipping over or from dripping paint onto the surface below it, fit the can into the broad side of an empty cereal or detergent box. Trace around the can and cut out a circle in the box that is exactly the right size for the can to sit in snugly.

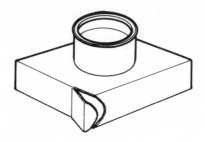

216 Save the paint

To insure an air-tight seal when you replace the lid on a paint can before storing it, brush a thin layer of paint into the groove the lid fits into. To avoid having a skin form on the top surface of the paint in a partly filled can, store the can upside down. With these two steps no air will reach the paint.

217 A visual painting record

Keep track of your paint jobs with a bar-chart made of tongue depressors, available at pharmacy or health supply stores. When a paint job is finished, dip one end of the stick into the paint about an inch. Let the paint dry and write on the rest of the stick the brand and color of the paint, the location of painted surface, the amount of paint required, and where the paint was purchased. Then mount the stick along with other stick records you've created in an area near your painting supplies.

218 Combing brushes

Any paint job risks being marred by loose brush bristles stuck in the painted surface. To remove loose bristles from a brush before painting, use a pocket comb reserved expressly for this purpose, or a metal-tooth animal comb available at pet supply stores.

219 Bagging brushes

If you want to stop painting for two or three hours, you don't have to go through all the work of cleaning your brush or roller and putting away your paint. Simply seal them tightly in a large plastic bag and they'll still be wet when you return. If your paint job extends over several days, wrap the brushes in aluminum foil, seal them tightly in plastic bags, and place them in the freezer between painting times. An hour or so before you're ready to paint again, take the bag out of the freezer and let the brush warm up before opening.

220 Cleaning a brush

To clean a paint brush, first brush it back and forth across sheets of newspaper or wipe it with newspaper to get as much paint off as possible. Then dip it repeatedly in lukewarm, soapy water while spreading and squeezing the bristles from the top of the brush downward. When the water dripping from the brush is clear, insert the bristles in a small but loosely fitting paper bag and then shake the bag and brush vigorously. This will get most of the moisture off the brush. Then remove the brush for final air drying.

221 Cleaning a roller

To clean a paint roller, first roll it back and forth across a few sheets of newspaper to remove as much paint as possible. Then run a small amount of liquid soap or detergent across the roller in a zig-zag line and wash the roller under running lukewarm water, gently wringing it throughout the procedure. When the water wrung from the roller is clear, rub the roller to raise the nap and stand it upright on a newspaper to dry. Never lay it flat while drying or it will develop a matted area on one side.

222 Bristle relaxer

No matter how well you clean a paintbrush, the bristles can get progressively stiffer as time goes by, whether they're natural or synthetic. Alleviate this condition by soaking your paint brushes in vinegar, for brushes used with water-based paint, or turpentine or paint thinner, for brushes used with oil-based paint, at least twenty minutes after cleaning them.

223 Storing brushes: long-term

When you've finished a painting job, clean each brush and store it in a small plastic bag with a half-teaspoon of turpentine or paint thinner, if the brush is used for oil-based paints, or vinegar, if the brush is used with water-based paints. Then fasten the bag tightly to the handle with a rubber band. The next time you paint, the brush will be soft and shapely.

224 Paint brush hanger

Storing paint brushes that are still damp (but not dripping) after cleaning is no problem on a homemade hanging rack. Cut a length of coat hanger for the rack itself. Bend one end into a loop that runs through a screw eye in the underside of a workshop shelf. Below this loop, make a dog-leg bend so that the rest of the coat hanger length will run about an inch-and-a-half below the underside of the shelf. Bend the other end of the coat hanger so that it can attach to a hook screwed into the underside of the shelf. To hang a brush, just unhook the end of the hanger and slide the brush on through the hole at the end of its handle. Just to be on the safe side, place something beneath the rack to catch any drips.

225 Restoring a rock-hard brush

Don't throw away an old paintbrush used with oil paint just because the bristles have become rock hard. You'll probably be able to restore the suppleness of the bristles completely by soaking the brush for a half an hour in a mixture of two tablespoons of salt, one cup of kerosene, and one quart of warm water.

226 A better first coat of varnish

To make the first coat of varnish adhere to a wood surface more strongly and evenly, thin it with 10 percent mineral spirits and rub it well into the wood, following the grain with your rubbing strokes. Then wait at least six hours before applying the next coat.

227 Keep varnish calm

Never agitate a varnish can or vigorously stir the contents. This will only make air bubbles that will blemish the finished surface. Varnish does not have any pigments or sediments that need to be blended.

228 Final refinishing polish

When you're through varnishing or staining, you can probably detect small drips and dust particles in your work—nothing serious, but still annoying. Get rid of these imperfections after the finish has dried with very fine (000 grade) steel wool dipped in wax polish. Rub the wool over the surface, using light strokes that follow the grain. Then buff with a clean cloth.

229 Speedy louver staining

Louvered doors or shutters are a nuisance to stain. Not only does it take a lot of time to cover all the wood surfaces with a brush, it also takes a lot of skill to make sure that the surfaces are covered evenly, without runs and pools. To stain louvers faster and more professionally, use a plastic bottle with a pump spray, such as the kind used for commercial glass cleaners. When you're through misting the wood with the stain, lightly wipe off the excess and then clean the bottle by spraying thinner through it.

230 Making nail holes disappear

Don't fill nail holes with putty before you stain or varnish wood trim, fill them afterward. If you fill them before, the putty will absorb the stain or varnish differently than the wood, making the holes even more noticeable. Also, try to drive trim nails in along the darker lines of the grain, where they will naturally be more concealed.

231 Aging the color of molding

Staining fresh molding to match the appearance of old molding is not easy. To approximate the original molding's aged color, first stain the new molding with a coat of golden oak stain, regardless of what type of wood or what color the new molding itself may be. Go on to apply one or more coats of the appropriate stain—the one used on the old molding—until the old and new molding match. The golden oak stain provides the "aging" ingredient you need to make the match.

232 Wallpaper sprayer

You may not need to rent a wallpaper steamer the next time you have to remove old wallpaper. First, try spraying the wallpaper with hot water in a paint sprayer. This way, it's easy to give tough spots extra attention. It helps to score the surface of the wallpaper with a sharp blade at frequent intervals so that the sprayed-on water can reach the paste more easily. When all the glue is noticeably soft, you can remove the paper with a wall scraper.

233 Wallcovering paste clean-up

Removing old, wet wallcovering paste from a wall doesn't have to be a messy task. Spray the paste with warm water to soften it. Then use a rubber-blade window squeegee to scrape off the paste and residue in quick easy strokes.

234 See where you've pasted

One of the secrets of a good wallcovering job is to make sure the back of each strip is completely covered with paste before you hang it. Clear or white paste makes this very hard to check. To see right away whether you've missed any spots, mix a dab of food coloring into the paste before you apply it. Just be careful not to add a lot of coloring or it may seep through. A very light tint will do.

235 Roller for pasting

A paint roller with a medium-depth nap makes an excellent substitute for a wallcovering paste brush. Pour the paste in the roller tray and run the roller through it just as you would with paint. Clean-up is as easy as it is with paint.

236 Built-in mildew protection

Sometimes mildew can form in dry wallcovering paste, weakening the bond and perhaps discoloring the covering. Some pastes are chemically treated to prevent this, but others aren't. To be on the safe side, spray Lysol or a similar disinfecting liquid on the paste side of the wallcovering as you put it up. It won't affect the consistency or effectiveness of the paste.

237 Pointing out anchor spots

Just before you recover the walls of a room, try this trick to mark where you've put wall anchors for heavy items like mirrors. Stick a piece of toothpick into each anchor hole so that the point sticks out about ½ inch. If the hole is too big to support a single toothpick, use two or more until there's a tight fit. When you put the covering over these holes, the toothpick points will penetrate the covering and tell you where the anchor spots are.

238 Plumb-good wallcovering job

To ensure that you hang wallcovering in a straight up-and-down line, the first length is critical. All others take their measure from it. Before you hang that first length, hang a plumb bob from the top of the wall almost all the way down to the floor. Then line up the first length with the plumb string. For a perfect job, use the plumb bob on each length. It won't take much extra time.

239 Bursting wall-covering bubbles

A common problem during a wallcovering job is the emergence of small bubbles in covering that you've already laid. To get rid of a very small bubble (less than ½ inch across), try sticking a pin in the center and forcing any underlying paste through the pinhole. If this doesn't work, or if the bubble is bigger, first slit the bubble with a razor blade crossways in an X over the center. Then peel back the edges and squirt some paste inside. Finally, smooth the edges over the paste. Don't worry about slight overlaps as they probably won't be noticeable after the paste has dried.

240 Touch-up squeezer

The next time you finish wallcovering a room, fill a cone-tipped plastic squeeze bottle (sold at drugstores and dime stores) with some leftover wallcovering paste. The odds are high that you'll find little spots over the next few days where the seams are not completely adhered. The squeezer will help you restick these spots in no time.

241 Tear that patch!

When you're making a wallcover patch to cover a small flaw or damaged area, try tearing the patch itself instead of cutting it. The ragged edge of a torn patch, assuming it feathers to the back of the paper, will be much less discernible once it's dried on the wall than the smooth edge of a cut patch.

242 Aging scrap wallcovering

For wallcover patch jobs to look good, the patch itself should be faded by the light and air like the paper on the wall. To achieve this, pin leftover wallcovering in a concealed area that's exposed to the sun, in an attic or on a storeroom wall, perhaps.

243 Cleaning wallcoverings

To clean marks or dirt off nonwashable wallcovering, use a rolled-up blob of rye bread or a kneaded eraser (available at art supply stores). Also, consider making the wallcovering washable by applying a transparent wallcovering coating. Try the effect of the coating on a leftover scrap ahead of time.

5

INTERIOR: FURNISHINGS, WALLS, FLOORS, CEILINGS

244 Stud detection without tools

If you need to locate the studs in a wall and you don't have any tools around for doing so, try rapping the wall with your knuckles, back and forth and up and down. A deep, hollow sound indicates a space between studs. A higher, less resonant sound indicates a stud. Also, look for nail holes in the baseboards (or for filler that partially conceals nail holes). The nails at the top of baseboards are almost always driven into studs. The nails at the bottom of baseboards, however, are apt to be driven into the toeplate of the wall.

245 Sheathing against the grain

When you need to install plywood sheathing against studs, it's better to install it so that the grain on the better quality surface runs perpendicular to the studs. That way, the wall will be significantly stronger.

246 Bridging panel gaps

Thin wall paneling has a tendency to shrink or shift due to humidity changes, leaving different colored gaps that are unsightly. Deal with this before you install the paneling. First, separate the panels and let them stand in the room for a few days before you put them on the walls so that they can adjust to the room's customary humidity. Second, paint a vertical strip on the stud or wall surface the same color as the paneling wherever two panels will meet. This way, if a gap forms between two panels in the future, it won't be visible.

247 Cut-out guide

Here's a quick and easy way to mark cut-out spots on sheets of paneling, plywood, or drywall that you're installing. First, draw a thin line of caulking on the outside edges of electrical switch and outlet boxes, and any other features that must come through the wall. Then press the sheet in place and tap it around the areas that need to be cut out. When you pull the sheet away, those places will be marked on the back by the caulking. If lipstick is available, use it instead of caulking for a more easily visible mark.

248 Back paneling with wallboard

Instead of nailing paneling onto bare studs, cover the studs with wallboard first. Then, use mastic to glue the paneling to the surface of the wallboard. The final wall will have no exposed nail heads and will be much more substantial. Furthermore, the paneling will never bow or warp.

249 Plaster repair secrets

Before plastering a large, shallow crater in a wall, insert staples randomly into the surface to be covered, especially in the bottom half of the crater. Make sure the staples stick out, but not beyond the finished surface you want. (If you're using a staple gun, tape a thin piece of wood—roughly the thickness of a tongue depressor—to the bottom of the staple gun and the staples won't go in all the way.) The protruding staples act as hoops for the filling compound to lock around and make the final bond much more secure.

250 Patching baseboard

When you have to patch two lengths of baseboard together, you'll get a better joint if you miter the two sections rather than butting their squared-off ends together. Cut the end of one board at a matching 45-degree angle that slants to the rear. Cut the end of the other board at a matching 45-degree angle that slants to the front. Overlap the slanted cuts when you fasten the boards in place. This is called a "scarf joint."

251 Fast hole-patching

Do you have a fist-sized hole in a drywall that you want to cover quickly and easily? Cut a piece of smooth-textured cloth that will overlap the hole about 2 inches and soak it in a solution of water-diluted patching compound. Then smooth the cloth over the hole. After it's dry, spread on a concentrated coat of compound and sand it lightly so that the surface and edges are smooth for painting.

252 A plasterer's friend

Most patching jobs don't call for much plaster or compound. The next time you have a patching job, remember that a plunger turned upside down makes a great container for mixing and transporting small amounts of patching material. After the job is done, the rubber suction cup is easy to clean and none the worse for wear.

253 Keeping plaster moist

To prevent plaster from drying out too quickly while you're working with it, mix in some white vinegar. Approximately two tablespoons per quart of plaster will ensure that it stays wet almost twice as long and won't have any effect on the quality of the plaster itself.

254 Patching a small hole

If you have a small wallboard hole to repair, here's a trick for patching it easily and securely:

1. Cut the hole to a clean shape, with no ragged edges.

2. Get a scrap piece of metal, perhaps the bottom of a metal can, that's bigger than the hole. Drill some ¼ -inch holes at random in it for patching compound to key into. Also punch two holes in the center, and run a foot-long length of wire through them.

3. Cut a slit extending out from both sides of the hole that is just big enough for the scrap to be slipped in sideways while you hold onto the wires.

4. Once the scrap is inside the wall, pull the ends of the wire so that the scrap lies flat against the back of the hole. Then twist the ends of the wire around a thin stick straddling the hole on the outside of the wall, so that the can lid will be held in place.

5. Spackle the hole, working compound around the stick and into the keying holes. Cover all of the backing plate but do not quite fill the hole to the level of the wall surface.

6. When the compound dries, untie the stick and cut the wires at the level of the patch.

7. Apply a second coat of compound to bring the patched area level with the surrounding wall surface.

255 Patching a large hole

If you have a large wallboard hole to repair, here's a good way to do it without having to apply multiple layers of spackle:

1. Cut a piece of scrap wallboard into a square that is a bit larger than the hole itself.

2. Lay this wallboard square on top of the hole, trace around it, and saw out the square you have just traced.

3. Cut a 1×3 or similar cleat that is 6 inches longer than the horizontal span of the hole you've just made. Insert it into the hole and hold it in place so

that it runs horizontally across the middle of the hole with 3 inches going behind the wall on all sides.

4. Insert screws through the wall and into the board on each side of the hole, turning the screws until they dig below the surface of the wallboard.

5. Spread compound on all four edges of the square patch and on the front of the board in the hole. Then fit the patch in the hole while the compound is still wet.

6. Drive a screw through the center of the patch into the cleat behind. When the compound dries, fill up any cracks around the patch and also cover the screwheads.

256 Smoothing drywall seams

Sanding drywall compound smooth at the seams can be a messy and awkward job. You can smooth the seams better and with less trouble by simultaneously dampening and rubbing them with a wet towel or sponge. This should fill in low spots, level high spots, and make the seams unnoticeable. If not, the seams will only need a very light sanding after they dry.

257 "Pastry tube" patching

Applying cement patching material to a basement wall can be messy and cumbersome. In addition, tubes of cement patch are quite expensive. Here's how to make the job easier and cheaper. Fill a heavy-duty zip-lock plastic bag with cement, seal it shut, then cut a hole an inch in diameter across one bottom corner. This gives you a homemade "pastry tube" that works just as well as the commercial cement patch tubes. Spray the crack or hole with water before squeezing the cement into it. Level the patch with a trowel or with your hand, covered with another plastic bag.

258 No-fuss tile removal

When replacing vinyl floor tiles, you don't have to risk scorching other tiles with a heat gun or damaging the subfloor. Simply lay a cloth over one of the tiles to be replaced and move a hot iron across the cloth with slow, even strokes. In a minute or two, you can remove the tile with no trouble or damage, and you can proceed to the next tile.

259 Patching vinyl flooring

To make a patch for vinyl flooring, first take a piece of leftover flooring, or flooring borrowed from a hidden spot such as underneath an appliance, and cut it into a square or rectangle that is at least an inch bigger than the damaged area all around. Place the patch over the damaged area, align it with the design on the floor, and tape it in position. Then, using a sharp utility knife held along a metal straightedge at a perfectly perpendicular angle, cut through both the patch and the flooring beneath it about ½-inch in from the edge of the patch. Remove the tape and the patch and pry out the flooring section you've just cut. Cut several strips of masking tape and, using the knife point, insert them partway under the undamaged flooring on all sides of the patch hole, with the sticky side of the tape facing up. Finally, fit the patch into place and press all edges of the patch firmly down on the tape.

260 Ending floor-board squeak

Often you can take the squeak out of a floorboard by sprinkling a dry lubricant into the adjacent board joints. Try talcum powder or furniture wax.

261 Budging a no-budge window

When all other means fail to open a window that is stuck closed, try this method. Screw a wood block to the lower portion of the sash. The block should be about 2 inches wide and 6 inches long, and the length should run parallel to the bottom of the sash no closer than 1½ inches away. Then place a second small board roughly the same size on the window sill. Finally, insert the end of a long board between the two blocks and use it as a lever to pry the sash upward.

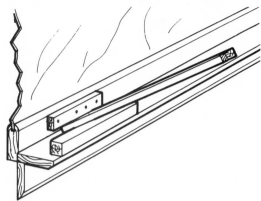

262 Window de-sticker

Don't force or pry into windows that are sticky or painted shut. Instead, run a pizza cutter back and forth in the groove that is sticky or paint-covered. This technique should free the window quickly and safely.

263 Sliding sash

If vertical or horizontal sliding sash move but only erratically and with difficulty, paint the tracks with a thin coating of petroleum jelly. Open and close the sash several times to spread the lubricant. Another good window lubricant is a near-liquid silicone gel (comes with a spongelike dauber).

264 Block that window

A piece of scrap wood wedged into the lower sash groove in the jamb of a double-hung window (behind the sash cord if necessary) makes an excellent, easy-to-remove security device. Cut it a few inches shorter than the groove itself so that the window can be opened for air but not sufficiently wide to admit an outsider.

265 Nail down window security

To secure a double-hung sash window against being forced open from the outside, use a stout nail as a locking mechanism. Standing on the inside, drill a downward-sloping hole for the nail where the rails meet the sash, at one side near the jamb. Drill all the way through the top rail of the bottom sash, and halfway into the bottom rail of the top sash. The hole should be big enough so that you can slip the nail in and out from the inside. When the nail is in place, intruders won't be able to see it nor will they be able to jiggle it out of its hole.

266 Seeing clearly

An effective window cleaner that has none of the drawbacks of ammonia or alcohol solutions is simply a cup of cornstarch in a gallon of warm water. Apply the solution with a sponge, wipe off with a dry cloth or paper towels.

267 Holding cracked glass in place

Cracked glass will stay put if you take care to apply transparent liquid cement to both sides of the glass, overlapping the crack by a half-inch on either side. The bond will make the repaired glass almost as strong as new glass, although you'll still be able to see the crack.

268 A cleaner seal

When glazing windows, skylights, or glass panels with silicone sealant, be sure to wear cotton or disposable plastic gloves. This will avoid creating fingerprints on the glass to which the sealant would stick.

269 Loosening windows

Got a window that's difficult to open and close? Try rubbing a block of paraffin or a candle on the inside of the vertical tracks. The waxy deposit may well provide sufficient lubrication for easier sliding action. If the window has sash cords, apply graphite dust (sold at hardware stores) to the pulley shafts on each side of the window.

270 Automatic door-sanding

A good way to unstick a door that rubs against a particular spot on the floor or on the door frame is to tape a piece of sandpaper to that spot. In the course of normal use, the door will sand itself down, at which point you can remove the sandpaper.

271 Shim for a sticking door

To correct a door that sticks, first determine *where* it sticks. You can do this by slipping a dollar bill between the door and the jamb, closing the door, and sliding the bill up and down or right and left to find where it can't pass. If it binds along the bottom, it may be because the bottom hinge is recessed too deeply into the frame of the door. Bring the hinge out by unscrewing the hinge leaf that fits in the frame, placing a piece of cardboard as a shim behind it, and rescrewing the hinge leaf through the cardboard. If the door sticks along the top, try the same procedure with the top hinge leaf.

272 Door straightening

As they age, doors can begin to bow in the center. To check for bowing, stretch a string taut from top to bottom across the face of the door. A bowed door will touch the center of the string on one side, and only the ends of a string on the other side. To straighten out a bowed door, lay it horizontally, supported just at the ends, with the unsupported bow facing upward. Then lay a couple concrete blocks across the bow's highest point (protect the door surface with a folded cloth). Leave the weights in place until a taut-string check shows that the door is straight again.

273 Lubricating sliding doors

Lubricate the tracks of sliding glass or wooden doors with graphite or silicone spray instead of oil. Oil will accumulate dirt, which can make it harder for the doors to slide smoothly.

274 Taking the swing out of doors

Bothered by a door that won't stay open when you want it to? Cut off the handle of an old toothbrush about an inch and a half from the bristles and drill two holes about an inch apart in the handle stub. Take down the door and screw the handle to the underside of the door, so that the brush faces downward. The next time you leave the door ajar, it will be held in place by the brush bristles flexed against the floor.

275 Taking the bang out of doors

Do you have a door that tends to slam shut with an explosive noise? Soften the blow with ⅛-inch thick tabs of foam rubber glued at intervals along the stop against which the door shuts. The tabs will cushion the slam of the door, and yet they're sufficiently flexible for the door to close easily.

276 New life for old doors

Be on the lookout for paneled doors at yard sales, auctions, and dumps. Not only can they be used as closet doors, they can also be cut in half through the horizontal rails and used as cabinet doors.

277 Hot solution for sticky drawers

Humidity in the air can swell a wooden drawer so that it sticks. To reduce the swelling, remove the drawer and place it in a warm oven for a few minutes. After the drawer has dried out, check to see if it now slides easily when you put the drawer back. If so, remove the drawer and coat it with wood preservative to prevent it from swelling again.

278 Fixing drawer glides

If a drawer has trouble closing all the way, it may be because the glides that support the drawer are badly worn. To lift the drawer front and keep it from hitting the frame as it closes, insert two or three smooth-headed thumbtacks into the top of each glide, toward the front, as shown.

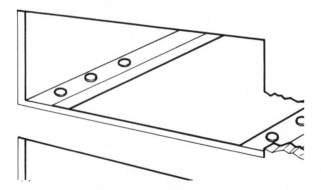

279 Damage-free molding removal

One of the initial steps in any flooring project is removing the molding. Using a small pry bar to pry the molding off the baseboard is commonly recommended, but this can scar and dent both the baseboard and the molding. A safer method is first to insert a putty knife between the molding and the baseboard. Then work a ⅛-inch thick scrap of wood between the knife blade and the baseboard. Finally, place the pry bar be-

tween the wood scrap and the knife blade and gently
pry the two apart.

280 Finding a match for old molding

Want to find an exact match when you're repairing or
supplementing old molding? You may be able to find
it inside a closet in the room. Remove that molding,
use it where you need it, and replace it inside the closet with any type of molding. The difference won't
matter there.

281 Magnetic access plates

Many houses have plywood plates over kitchen and
bathroom wall openings that provide access to the
plumbing pipes. Often, they're beneath the sink. Unfortunately, each plate is usually nailed onto the studs
and has to be pried off whenever you need to work on
a pipe. The next time you have to do this, mount strip
magnets on the corners of the plywood plate and
mount metal tabs on the studs where the magnets can
connect. Then just align the magnets with the metal
tabs and forget nailing the plate to the stud. The plate
will remain in place and yet be easy to remove without the risk of disfiguring the plate and the wall.

282 Dust-free drilling

To avoid spilling dust when you're drilling into a gyp-
sum board or plaster ceiling, first run the drill through
the lid of a plastic food container. When the drill is
aimed upward, the lid will rest against the chuck with
the rim projecting toward the tip of the drill. In this position, the lid functions as a perfect dust collector.

283 Drill bit guide

For a drill bit guide, use a block of wood with a hole
drilled into it the same diameter as the bit. Stick it to

the surface with rubber cement. After drilling, the guide can easily be removed with just a little prying. You can make drill bit guides of this kind for vertical or angular alignments of the bit, or to stop the bit at a desired depth.

284 Sticky solution

To prevent screws, nuts, and washers from falling in your face when you're installing an overhead fixture, give them a light coating of rubber cement or tacky glue. This will keep them attached to the screwdriver or wrench. Once in place, it's easy to wipe the glue from all affected surfaces.

285 Screw hammering

As a general rule, it's not a good idea to hammer a screw. However, giving a screw a few taps with a hammer before the last couple of twists will give the threads a better bite into the wood. The taps force the wood fibers to compress and slant downward against the threads.

286 A tighter fit for screws

Is a hole too large for the screw that needs to be there? Place one or more glue-smeared matchsticks or toothpicks in the hole to give the screw threads something to bite into.

287 Sawing plywood: a cleaner cut

It's difficult to saw through plywood without creating a splintery edge. You can avoid this by laying a strip of masking tape along your intended cutting line on the finished side before you mark it. Saw through the marked tape, peel it off, and admire the result.

288 Cutting plywood sheets

To provide convenient support while cutting large sheets of plywood, create a temporary workbench out of sturdy cardboard boxes that are all the same size (preferably about 30 inches high). You can simply stack them together or you can bind them together with strong tape. Then lay the plywood sheet across the top of the box-platform for sawing. It won't make any difference that you'll also be sawing into the boxes themselves.

289 Cutting cross-grain materials

When cutting cross-grain on the face of plywood, a lauan mahogany door, or any other finished wood surface, first score the line to be cut with a utility knife. Then run the saw blade along the outside of the scored line. The scored line will prevent the edge from splintering.

290 Keeping an open cut

Want to prevent your saw from getting stuck in the wood as it cuts through it? Insert a screwdriver into the kerf behind the blade to keep the two sides sufficiently apart.

291 Head start for cutting metal

Starting a hacksaw into a piece of thin metal isn't easy. The saw tends to skip along the edge instead of cutting into it. Give it some help by nicking the edge of the metal with a file at the exact point where you want it cut.

292 A clean cut

Before you cut a bolt or some other threaded piece of hardware, screw on a nut to a position just one or two threads above where you want to cut. This way, you'll keep the saw blade from accidentally damaging the rest of the bolt, and you'll clean the cut threads when you unscrew the nut.

293 No-split nails

Thin pieces of wood, such as moldings, can easily split when they're nailed. Keep this from happening by blunting the pointed tip of each nail with a few hammer taps before you use it. The newly blunted tip will then push through the wood rather than splitting it.

294 Hammering in reverse

You don't have to fumble around with two hands trying to hammer a nail into a small, hard-to-reach place. Just wedge the nail between the claws of the hammer with the head of the nail braced against the base of the hammer. Pound the nail in "backwards" until it's securely in the wood. Then lift the hammer off the nail, turn it around, and continue hammering the normal way.

295 Disappearing finishing nail

Want to keep the head of a finishing nail from showing? After it's been nailed into the wood, use another nail as a nail set. Then fill the indentation with wood putty.

296 Easier mortise cuts

Whenever you have to make a pocket or mortise cut in the edge of wood, first scribe the outline clearly with a sharp knife. Then, with the chisel, make several closely spaced cuts crosswise within the scribed outline, beginning with a cut at one end and working to the other end. It's safer to chisel out each small section one at a time than the whole section at once.

297 Homemade nailing guard

To avoid leaving hammer marks on pieces of wood you are nailing, make a nail guide and holder. Cut one or more slots the same width as the nail diameter in a scrap piece of ¼- or ½-inch plywood, or ⅛-inch sheet of aluminum. The guide shown has a slot at a pointed end for working in corners, and two slots of different depths along one side to space nails evenly across the width of flooring or siding. To use the holder as a protector, start the nail with a tap or two, slip the holder into place around it, and drive the nail in, stopping just at the point where you can slip the holder free. Then use a nail set to drive the nail flush with or below the finish surface. To make a guard/holder for nails of any diameter, make V-shaped cutouts instead of narrow slots.

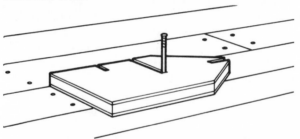

298 Washer-and-nut bonding

A recurring problem for any home do-it-yourselfer is trying to put a washer and nut onto a bolt in a blind spot. To eliminate some of the frustration, first bond the washer to the nut with a couple of dabs of rubber cement, then you're ready to put the washer-nut combination onto the bolt.

299 Finger fastener

Keeping hold of a nut in a tight space is always frustrating and often impossible without a magic touch. The next time you're faced with this dilemma, make a tiny ring out of duct tape with the sticky side facing out and attach it to the end of your finger. Then pick up the nut with that finger and place it anywhere your finger can reach.

300 A wooly bite for glue

Whenever you're gluing a joint together, sprinkle several strands of steel wool over the glue-covered surface before clamping the two pieces together. This will help the two pieces to stay together while the glue dries and to bond more tightly after drying.

301 Coming unglued

Glue often spreads from a newly made joint to surrounding surfaces, where it creates annoying lumps or stains. Minimize this problem by running strips of plastic tape along both sides of the joint to be glued. Then apply the glue, assemble the pieces, and wait for the glue to dry. Afterward, you can peel away the tape to get rid of any excess glue. Run a knife along the joint to strip away any ridge of glue that's accumulated there. Use the same approach when caulking around cabinets or countertops.

302 Clean clamping

Worried about whether a clamp will get stuck to a wooden joint that you're about to glue? Before applying the clamp, wrap a sheet of waxed paper around the joint and clamp over it.

303 Leg clamp

A screw-tightening automobile hose clamp makes an ideal clamp for round pieces of broken or split wood, like furniture legs. It offers tight, uniform pressure while the glue or cement dries. Be sure to tighten the clamp over a piece of cloth to avoid harming the wood. You can purchase the clamps in several diameters.

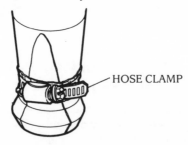

HOSE CLAMP

304 Restoring plastic wood

To keep plastic wood from drying out while you're working with it, mix in a small amount of polish remover or lighter fluid. As long as the amount isn't too great, it won't have any effect on the plastic wood's bonding strength or appearance.

305 Putty pick

The next time you pass by a music store, drop in and buy a few cheap plastic guitar picks. Then, when you need to apply putty to a small nick in your woodwork or furniture, use one of these picks instead of a putty knife. The pick is smaller and more flexible, which means you will have less putty to clean or sand.

306 Popping out dents

Remove a dent from a wooden surface with an iron and a wet cloth. First, smooth the wet cloth over the dent. Then press the cloth with the iron set on "high." The dent will disappear almost immediately.

307 Small-scale sanding

If you have a piece of wood to sand that's hand-sized or smaller, it makes more sense to rub the piece against the sandpaper rather than vice versa. Fasten a full sheet of sandpaper to a clipboard, using additional spring clips on each side to hold it in place. This gives you a secure, reusable sanding surface.

308 Folding sandpaper

Sandpaper is quite brittle and therefore hard to fold to an exact size. Before attempting to fold it, run the smooth side back and forth over the edge of your workbench. This will create tiny fractures all across the adhesive layer, which won't affect the strength of the sandpaper but will make it much easier to fold.

309 Sandpaper reinforcement

Fine-grit sandpaper on a mechanical sander or a sanding block has a tendency to tear before it wears out. To prevent this from happening, apply self-adhesive contact paper to the back of the sandpaper.

310 Seat-of-your-pants polishing

Don't throw out an old pair of jeans. Instead, cut it into pieces, avoiding any seams. Use the denim scraps for very fine jobs, such as the last round of polishing on oiled, varnished, or lacquered wood. When you've finished this "sanding," use a damp cloth to pick up any remaining dust.

311 Two-ladder scaffold

Moving a stepladder along with you as you go from one work spot to another is tiresome. If you have 3 stepladders, you can create a scaffold to walk along by positioning the ladders several feet apart, facing each other, and bridging opposite steps with a stout, wide board. For safety, be sure to tie or clamp the board to the steps on which it rests.

312 Stepladder security

Keep your stepladder from accidentally toppling over by equipping it with temporary outrigger braces. Use C-clamps to attach wooden struts to both back legs of the ladder so that they touch the floor 2 or 3 feet at either side. If you need to get close to a wall, remove the outrigger on that side. The taller the stepladder, the more you need this protection, especially on an uneven floor.

313 Cola cure for rusted hardware

If you have a blot that's rusted into a nut, or if you have a rusty screw, throw it into a glass of carbonated cola. After a few hours, remove it from the glass and you'll probably find it clean of rust.

314 Substitutes for penetrating oil

Out of penetrating oil to cut through rust or corrosion? Tincture of iodine is a good substitute, but be careful not to get it on anything that would stain. Other effective substitutes are lemon juice, hydrogen peroxide, and kerosene.

315 Kitchen-safe lubrication

When lubricating kitchen appliances, eliminate the need to worry about whether the oil might come in contact with your food. Use mineral oil or glycerin purchased at the drugstore. It will work just as well, and it won't pose any health or taste threat to your food.

316 Screw tape

When you are taking apart an item that must be re-assembled, don't lose track of the screws that hold it together. Insert them into the little tunnels along the cut edge of a piece of corrugated cardboard—like slipping bullets into a cartridge belt. Or, lay the screws side by side on a piece of cardboard and run a piece of tape across them, pressing it down to the cardboard on both sides of each screw—again much like a cartridge belt. Tape the cardboard to a major part of the item so it won't get lost before reassembly.

317 Labeling motor parts

Anytime you're working on a motor, be sure to label everything you disconnect, so that you can make re-connections correctly. Use a tiny brush to paint matching numbers on large items that go together. Color-code smaller connections. Attach masking-tape tags to wires and label or code them with a permanent felt-tip marker.

318 Compound squeeze

When you're using compound from a tube, don't assume that it's properly mixed. Always squeeze the tube from top to bottom a couple of times to blend the contents before removing the top. It could save you unwanted trouble later on.

319 Removing mastic from walls

The mastic used to glue anything plastic (such as tiles) onto the wall is notoriously difficult to remove, even though the plastic item itself will come off with very little effort. To remove the mastic, first soften it with a hair dryer, then scrape it off with a putty knife. Assuming you are removing old plastic tiles that you want to replace with new ones, or with ceramic tiles, it isn't necessary to remove all the old mastic. As long as the scraped surface is reasonably smooth, the new layer of mastic will make up for minor surface variations of the old dried mastic.

320 Plastic bucket repair

Don't throw out a plastic bucket just because it has cracked and developed a leak. Instead, repair the bucket with a table knife and a lighted candle. Use the candle flame to warm up the knife blade and then press the blade against the crack, rubbing slowly back and forth. The heat generated by the knife will melt the plastic just enough to repair the crack.

321 Rot patrol

Periodically check the wood framing of your house for wood rot. Prod any bleached-out or brown patches with an icepick. If they are splintery or spongy, scour them with a wire brush and then rub common salt into the wood. This should get rid of the fungus that's causing the rot.

322 Testing wetness in the basement

If you suspect that you have a dampness problem in your basement, try this simple test. Tape large squares of aluminum foil to various random spots on the basement walls and floor, making sure to seal all four sides of each square so that it won't vent. Two days later, examine both sides of each square. If the side of the foil facing the wall or floor is wet, you have a seepage problem. If the side of the foil facing into the room is wet, you have a condensation problem.

323 Moisture dampers

Basement dampness is due to seepage, to condensation, or to both.

Here are some ways to prevent seepage:

- Make sure all downspouts and gutters are at least 8 feet away from the foundation and that they empty water into storm drains.
- Coat the walls and floors of the basement with waterproofing paint.
- Repair all cracks in the walls and the floors with hydraulic cement.

Here are some ways to prevent condensation:

- Install a dehumidifier in the basement.
- Repair all plumbing leaks.
- Insulate all cold water pipes.
- Trim trees and plants away from outside the basement walls in order to permit better air and light circulation.

324 De-flash flashing

Metal flashing around visible fixtures (such as heating and water pipes, vents, range hoods, or air conditioners) is unsightly unless you paint it the same color as the surrounding surface. Unfortunately, it's tricky getting paint that's meant for walls or ceilings to stick to a metal surface and to dry smoothly. Here's a suggestion. Before you paint the metal, coat it with vinegar and then wipe off the vinegar. This will etch the metal slightly, rendering it more likely to hold paint. Next, apply a primer coat. Then paint the flashing the desired color.

325 Check system for asbestos

Asbestos sheeting may have been used in a number of places inside your home: in ceiling tiles, in the flooring, or in insulating materials. If an asbestos surface appears to be crumbly or to be giving off chalky deposits, don't try to clean it yourself and don't ignore it. Seek professional advice.

326 Curing a musty closet

If a closet with a solid door has a musty smell or noticeable mildew spots, the only way to solve the problem is to encourage better air circulation. Put a vent into the door or, better yet, replace the door with a louvered door.

327 Attic insulation check

To check if your attic is leaking heat, go outside several hours after a snowfall and see if the snow is melting in some spots more than others. Early melting spots are a sign of warm spots that are probably due to missing, damaged, or insufficient insulation just below.

328 Add attic insulation

In the typical attic, insulation is installed between the joists, and the top of the insulation is level with the top of the attic floor joists. If this is how your attic insulation was installed and you want to add a second layer, the new insulation will be more effective if you lay it at right angles across the joists.

329 Attic-hatch insulation

The attic hatch itself is often overlooked when it comes to insulating the house. Make sure your attic hatch is well insulated on top and weatherstripped around the edges.

330 Cleaner cut for insulation

Cutting insulation batts with regular scissors or knives can be arduous, uncomfortable, and even unsafe. Use manual hedge clippers or a serrated kitchen knife instead. And always wear gloves!

331 Bug out

Don't let ants drive you up the wall. Wipe or spray counters, cabinets, and floors with a solution of equal parts water and white vinegar.

332 Ice-smooth caulking

To smooth and shape a newly applied bead of caulking, run an ice cube over it. The ice will even out any lumps and give the caulking a pit-free surface.

333 Hinge repair with body putty

One way to tighten a loose hinge without disturbing the surrounding frame is to use automobile body putty. Remove the hinge from the jamb and fill the screw holes with the putty, using a putty knife. Mark the wet putty with a nail to show where the centers of the screw holes are. When the putty has dried, drill pilot holes for the screws and reinstall the hinge.

6

EXTERIOR: WINDOWS, SIDINGS, ROOFS, PROPERTY

334 Safe solution for mildew

Bothered by mildew on your deck, fence, shed, or roof? Scrub the affected areas with straight vinegar or a 50/50 solution of bleach and water. Then give them two coats of wood sealer.

335 Grease release

To get rid of grease stains from a concrete or patio-block terrace, use a poultice made of mineral spirits and whiting, both available at hardware stores. Spread it thickly over the stained area. When dry, brush it off. Repeat if necessary.

336 Repairing a stained chimney

When brown stains appear on the outside of a chimney—either defining the brick courses, outlining the concrete blocks, or dripping down the stucco—it's because the inner lining of the chimney is leaking creosote from the wood you're burning. This could be very dangerous, causing a fire or a chimney collapse. Before using the chimney again, have the flue cleaned and a liner installed. Cover the stains with an aluminum sealer and repaint.

337 An old shake for new shakes

To make new cedar shakes (shingles) match the old, weathered ones when you're repairing a roof, "age" them in the following manner. Combine a one-pound package of baking soda with a half gallon of water. Then brush or spray this mixture on the new shakes. Over three or four hours, they'll assume a permanent gray color.

338 Moss-buster

Here's how to get rid of moss from a brick patio, walkway, or wall. First, soak the bricks thoroughly with water. Next, apply a weedkiller, making sure to wear thick rubber gloves and to follow the manufacturer's directions carefully. Let the weedkiller sit on the bricks for five minutes, then scrub the bricks vigorously with a stiff, nylon bristle brush. Rinse afterward.

339 Window frame rescue

If your window frames are weatherbeaten but otherwise in fairly good shape, here's how to revive them. First, sand off any old paint. Then seal the wood with two coats of a homemade sealer: one part boiled linseed oil to one part paint thinner. Allow 24 hours between coats and three days after the last coat. Then, sand lightly, apply a primer, and paint.

340 Painless pane removal

Tapping out a broken window pane can be messy, if not dangerous. To eliminate the muss and fuss, secure the broken pane on both sides with cross-strips of duct or masking tape that remain within the borders of the pane. Then run one strip of tape across the middle of the broken pane and onto another pane or a wooden frame to function as a handle. This prevents the broken pane from falling out later. Gently tap the edges of the broken pane with a hammer and remove the entire pane easily and safely by pulling back the handle strip.

341 Invisible screen patch

To fix a small tear or hole in a window or door screen, use a scrap piece of screen and some clear caulking, such as silicone caulking. Begin by cutting around the damaged area so that all the edges are clean and flat. Then cut the scrap piece of screen slightly larger than the damaged area. Apply caulking to the edges of the patch and place it over the hole, so that the caulking can squeeze through the mesh of both pieces, forming keys that hold them together. Clean off any excess. Within two days, the caulking will have become completely transparent and the repair will be virtually unnoticeable.

342 Marking screens and storms

Mark all your screens and storm windows so that you'll know at a glance on which window frames they belong. Using a staple gun, make a Roman numeral with staples on each window frame and matching numerals on the corresponding screen and storm windows.

343 Swinging window boxes

Fasten your window boxes to the sill, wall, or railing with loose-pin hinges. This enables you to take down the boxes simply by pulling the hinge pins, so that you can more easily work on the flowers, move the boxes elsewhere (outdoors or indoors), and repair or paint the surfaces behind the boxes.

344 New twist for a gutter

Need to raise the pitch of a strap-supported gutter? You can do this quickly, easily, and effectively simply by twisting the strap with a pair of pliers. The more you twist, the shorter the strap becomes and the higher the gutter will rise.

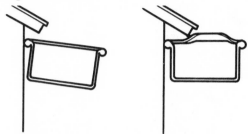

345 Seeing where the gutter sags

To check for sagging places in a gutter, run water slowly along the gutter from a hand-held garden hose. Note where the water collects in pools. Then inspect these areas to determine what correction needs to made in the adjacent hangers or brackets to keep the water running smoothly.

346 Signs of gutter trouble

If you notice a slight depression in the ground just beneath the gutter, chances are good that it was formed by water dripping from the gutter. Check the gutter at this point for a sag or a leak. Another sign of a possible sag or leak is the presence of icicles along the eave.

347 Leaf guard for gutters

Keep leaves from clogging your gutters and down-spouts. After making sure the gutters and downspouts are clean, cover the tops of them with large-mesh wire

screen, commonly called hardware cloth, which has
¼-inch or ⅜-inch square openings. Rain water will still
be able to run into your gutters and downspouts but
solid debris won't.

348 Better gutter repair

To seal gaps and small cracks in a rain gutter, use
screening and spray-on automobile undercoating. To
patch a hole in a rain gutter, first cover it with a piece
of screen and then spray the screen and the gutter
with undercoating.

349 Homemade gutter cleaner

A gutter that's too high to reach comfortably on a
ladder can be cleaned out with the help of a homemade cleaning tool. Use a 1×2 or 2×2 for the handle,
long enough to reach about a foot above the gutter.
Nail a piece of wood about 14 inches long to it at an
angle, and nail a brace between them to form an "A"
with the handle as a long leg. Remove the top from a
tin can and cut the can in half lengthwise to make a
scoop; leave the bottom uncut. Screw the bottom of
the can to the short leg of the A as shown. Now you
can walk along and scoop debris out of the gutter
overhead with ease.

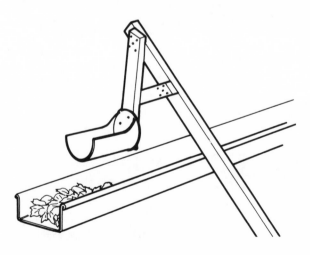

350 Reaming downspouts

A safe and easy way to clean debris out of gutter downspouts is to use a plumber's snake and work your way up from the bottom. The goal is to get the debris to loosen and fall downward out of the gutter. If the snake is unable to get through bends in the gutter, run a garden hose up the gutter and turn on the water full force.

351 Gentle-release downspout

It's a good idea to add a 3-foot extension to the elbow at the bottom of a downspout so that rain water doesn't empty right alongside the house itself. But a big gush of water emptying from the extension can still damage the surrounding ground surface. Solve this problem by drilling small holes all along the sides of the extension, so that the rain water squirts thinly from all the holes, thus dispersing itself more gently over a much bigger area.

352 Lifeline at the roofline

Don't risk tumbling to the ground while you're working on the roof. Always tie one end of a strong rope around your waist and the other end around the chimney or some other sturdy, fixed object.

353 Trailing a leak

When you notice a water spot on the ceiling, don't assume that the leak in the roof is directly above it. Most likely, water is leaking through at a higher spot and is running down the roof framing for a short stretch before dropping to the ceiling. The next time it rains, look underneath the roof for this type of trail. When you find the leak itself, poke a nail or wire up through it to help you locate it when you're on the roof. If you don't want to wait for rain, and don't mind possibly having to get on the roof, run a hose to the roof and water the area you want to inspect.

354 Patching small roofing holes

Most holes you'll find in routine checks of your roofing or flashing will be less than the size of a nickel. You can patch these holes simply by covering them with a layer of roof cement.

355 Shingle patching

When you need to repair an asphalt or asbestos shingle, use an appropriately sized rectangle of sheet copper or aluminum. First, coat one side of the metal rectangle with roofing cement. Then slide the metal beneath the damaged shingle, cement side down. Finally, apply roofing cement to the top of the metal piece and press the shingle down on top of it.

356 Rooftop bagging

The next time you're tearing off old roofing, stash the discarded pieces as you go along in double-thick, large plastic trash bags. It's safer, less messy, and much more efficient than throwing the pieces on the ground and picking them up later. It also minimizes the risk of stepping on roofing nails when cleaning up. When a bag is full, seal it with tape and carefully drop it to the ground, or lower it with a rope.

357 Is the tar out tonight?

Kerosene is the best solvent to remove tar or roofing cement from tools. An effective substitute is oleo. That's hardly practical or economical for tools, of course, but excellent to clean your hands or remove anything that's gotten into your hair. It is not harsh, and washes away with soap and water, leaving no odor or residue.

358 Handling a ladder

You can harm yourself, other people, or your property if you don't handle a tall ladder properly. Always carry it upright, with one side rail braced against your chest and one thigh. Grip a thigh-level rung from one side, and a head-high rung from the other side, as shown. To set the ladder you are carrying in place, stop about 2 feet from the wall it will rest against and turn sideways, so the ladder faces the wall. Lower the bottom of the ladder to the ground, then let the top gently come to rest against the wall. If you are using an extension ladder, extend the upper section now to about 6 inches above the final point you want it to rest. Finally, pull the bottom of the ladder out from the wall to a distance that is about one-fourth the extended length of the ladder. The top will move down a few inches as you do this.

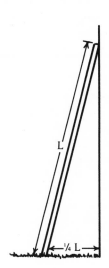

359 Ladder covers

The ends of a ladder can easily mark or gouge the wall against which they're leaning. To prevent this, cover the ends with rags folded into thick pads. Tie the pads to the ladder ends with plastic cord.

360 Anchoring a ladder

Ladders are unstable. Here are some tips for making your ladder more secure while you are working on it:

- Tie the side rails to outlying stakes in the ground between the ladder and the wall.

- Secure the ladder near the top by lashing it to a 2×4 held across the inside of a window frame. This 2×4 should be 1 foot wider than the window on each side, and its ends should be padded to prevent damage to the inside wall.

- The upper section of a ladder should overlap the lower section by at least one-quarter of its length.

361 Ladder strap

The next time you're working on a tall ladder that's resting against a scaffold, run a metal pipe strap around a top rung and secure the two ends of the strap to the scaffold with a C-clamp. That way, the ladder can't accidentally slide or be pushed away.

362 Ladder in a window

When the top of a ladder must rest in the center of a window opening, don't risk denting the sill with the rails, or poking the top through the glass as you position the ladder. Instead, tie a 2×4 that is 2 feet wider than the window opening to the top ends of the rails. It will span the opening and rest on the window frame or siding on either side. Pad the 2×4 if you want to protect the surface it will rest against.

363 Ladder scraper

Make your ladder safer with a scrap of burlap stapled tightly around the bottom rung. It will function as a shoe-scraper, preventing you from slipping on mud or moisture that dirty shoes might otherwise carry to higher rungs.

364 Ladder lubing

To keep wooden ladders from drying out and becoming dangerously brittle or splintery, paint them with linseed oil or varnish them on a routine basis. Give two coats to the rungs, which receive the most abuse.

365 Drive-away grime

To keep your concrete or blacktop driveway attractive and in good condition, regularly clean it in the following manner. Hose it down until it's completely wet. Coat it with a thin layer of nonpolluting detergent. Brush the detergent into the driveway surface with a broom. Rinse the driveway until the water runs clear.

366 Oil stain removal

Oil stains on a paved driveway or a concrete garage floor are notoriously difficult to clean. Try a solution of three tablespoons of lye per gallon of water. Brush it into the stain, let it stand for a half an hour, brush it again, and rinse it off. Dissolve the lye in cold—not warm or hot—water, and be sure to wear tightly sealed protective gloves.

367 Oil stain prevention

To prevent oil from staining a garage floor, make your own highly effective concrete sealer by mixing equal parts of kerosene and boiled linseed oil. Brush this mixture onto the concrete surface, making sure in advance that the surface is clean and dry. One hour later, wipe off any wet spots with a dry cloth.

368 Garage car stops

You can make sure that you never hit the back wall of your garage with your car, whether you're driving forward or backward. First, get two wooden blocks about 3×3×24 inches to use as wheel-stoppers and bore two bolt holes through each of them. Then bore larger-sized bolt holes 3 inches deep into corresponding spots on the garage floor, located so that each block will stop one of the car wheels before it hits the back wall. Six-inch bolts running through the holes in the wooden blocks into the holes in the floor will keep them in place, but because the floor holes are bigger than the bolts, you can remove the wheel-stoppers anytime you want.

369 Garage mirrors to check lights

Want to make sure that your car lights are functioning properly when you drive out of your garage at night? Put up a mirror at an inside front corner of your garage, and another mirror at an inside back corner. Position them so you can see the headlights in one mirror when you're sitting in the driver's seat, and can see the taillights in the other mirror when you look at the rearview or side mirror of the car.

370 Organizing your garage space

If your garage is always cluttered with tools, bikes, garden equipment, sports gear, and trash, a good first step toward getting things more organized is to paint lines on the garage floor that clearly indicate areas reserved for different storage purposes. The painted lines should be a highly visible color, such as yellow, and should be coated with shellac or clear varnish so that they'll wear longer.

371 Garage door weatherstripping

Cold air and debris can get inside a garage through the gap between the garage door and the floor. Weatherstrip this gap with a section of garden hose that's as long as the door. Just slit it lengthwise in a straight line, fit it around the door bottom and secure it with a few well-spaced nails.

372 No-stick mow or snow

You don't have to wait for a wet lawn to dry before mowing it. Just coat the blades of your mower with vegetable oil; apply the oil with a brush, or with a plant sprayer. Wet grass clippings will slide right off. The same procedure keeps snow from sticking to a snow shovel or clogging a snow blower. An alternative to vegetable oil is furniture spray wax. Think twice about wet mowing, however: If you use a mower-attached bag to collect clippings, you may prefer to wait until the lawn is dry before mowing. Wet grass in a bag can be bothersome.

373 Lawn mower guard

Make your own lawn mower guard to protect yourself from accidentally putting your foot underneath the mower or being hit by flying rock fragments. Cut a piece of flat sheet metal approximately 5x20 inches (depending on the size of your mower). Attach this piece to the back of your mower with a strap hinge at either end, so that it hangs ½-inch from the ground. The strap hinges will allow the piece of sheet metal to swing back for tall grass.

374 A well-planted hose coil

A large plastic plant pot can be made into a hanger for a garden hose. Attach the bottom of the pot to the side of the house or garage with 2-inch drywall screws and large washers. When you've finished with the hose, simply coil it around the planter and keep the nozzle and any other attachments inside the planter. The slope of the planter side will hold the coil snugly against the wall.

375 A sharper chain saw

A sharp chain saw works faster and more smoothly than a dull one, but a chain saw dulls so gradually that it's difficult to tell when it needs to be sharpened. If you see that it's producing sawdust rather than chips, the time has come.

376 Squeezer for chain saw oil

Tired of having to use a funnel to oil your chain saw, or of having to put up with the inevitable spillage? The job can be done more easily and neatly if you store your chain saw oil in a cone-tipped plastic squeeze bottle, widely available in grocery and dime stores.

377 Winterizing garden tools

Before you put your gardening tools away for the winter, be sure to winterize them. First, remove any dirt. Then give the wooden parts a light coat of linseed oil, and the metal parts a light coat of floor wax. This technique will prevent the wood from drying out and the metal from corroding.

378 Mower winterizing

To ensure the long-term effectiveness of your mower, take care to winterize it properly between grass-cutting seasons. Drain all the gas. Then run the engine to eliminate the last few drops of gas that are still likely to remain in the tank. Take out the spark plug and give the cylinder a couple of squirts of oil. Pull the starter cord two or three times to distribute the oil inside the cylinder before putting the spark plug back in. Drain the oil from the crankcase.

379 Winter seeding

You don't have to wait for warm weather to do something about the bare spots on your lawn. Lay fresh seed on them during late winter thaws. As the soil thaws and refreezes, it will crumble itself into an ideal seedbed and your lawn will look better faster.

380 Scaring birds off a new lawn

To avoid having birds eat up your newly laid lawn seed, run string from stake to stake around and across the seeded area. Then attach 1-inch by 1-foot strips of aluminum foil to the string every 1½ feet. These strips will twist and flash in the air in even just a gentle breeze, which will discourage birds from coming anywhere near.

381 Aerate as you walk

While you're mowing the lawn, you can simultaneously aerate and loosen the soil, which will make it much more fertile and water-retentive. Just wear strap-on "spiker" shoes for the occasion. Available at most nurseries and gardening supply stores, spiker shoes have thin spikes pointing perpendicularly from the bottom that poke holes in the soil as you walk on it.

382 Mow, mow, mow your lawn

Change directions every time you mow your lawn to avoid repeating the same cutting pattern and thereby giving your lawn a streaky look. To make your lawn look particularly good for a special occasion, mow it twice, in different directions. This helps guarantee that every blade will be square-cut and identical in height.

383 Dirt collector for planting

Any time you're about to dig a hole to plant a tree, shrub, or large specimen plant, spread out a plastic or burlap sheet right next to the spot where you'll be digging. As you dig, throw the dirt onto this sheet. When you're finished, you can refill the hole simply by picking up one side of the sheet and dumping the dirt back into the hole. The surrounding lawn will remain clean and any leftover dirt can easily be carried away.

384 Lawn de-mole-ition

Are moles tunneling under your lawn and ruining it? If so, then your lawn is full of grubs as well. Get rid of the grubs with a relatively safe insecticide like diazinon or chlorpyrifos and you also get rid of the moles.

385 Post-snowplow cleanup

If you live where there is a lot of snow accumulation in the winter, by spring the edge of your lawn next to the street is likely to be full of debris left by snowplowing. To keep such debris from ruining the lawn, secure sheets of clear plastic over the lawn when snow first seems likely—after the first frost. Covering a strip about 3 feet wide should be sufficient. In the spring, simply roll up the plastic to get rid of the debris.

386 Tree circles

The roots of a tree will be better nourished by rainfall if you keep the area around the trunk free of grass and the earth well spaded to remain loose and easily penetrated by water. To make sure that the area you clear is attractively circular, tie a rope in a loop that goes around the shovel handle (just above the blade) and the tree trunk. Adjust the loop size so that when it is pulled tight the shovel will be at the edge of your intended circle. As you dig around the tree, the loop will keep you on course.

387 Burlap tree-saver

Save young trees from being eaten alive by rabbits and other small bark-loving animals. Wrap burlap around the trunk to a height of about 3 feet. Be sure to tie the burlap or clip it with spring-type clothes pins, but don't staple or nail it. Any puncture wounds provide decay and disease access.

388 Deer-departed shrubs

Hungry deer can do a great deal of damage to your shrubbery during the winter months, especially when the weather turns extra cold and the ground is covered with snow or ice. Here's a trick that will make your shrubbery much less attractive to deer. Hang nylon stockings or panty hose legs stuffed with hair clippings (available from barber and beauty shops) or bar soap (not deodorant, perfumed, or lotion-containing soap) from random shrubbery branches. The filled stockings or panty hose legs should be tucked into the shrubbery so that they'll stay in place and won't be too unsightly.

389 From dust to mulch

The next time you're about to throw away a pile of sawdust or chips from chain-sawing, spread it around your flower beds instead. Sawdust makes an effective and attractive mulch.

390 Critter-proof flower beds

Want to discourage cats, dogs, and other four-footed visitors from messing up your flower beds or bothering your trees? Mix moth balls or flakes into the dirt surrounding beds and trees. This will also keep garden snakes and many varieties of insects away.

391 Outdoor chair drain

Rainwater collects in the seats of metal patio chairs, which generally have built-in contour curves. If the water is left there, the seat will start to rust. Keep this from happening by drilling two or three small holes in the lowest spots of each chair seat. Water will drain right through, and the holes won't disturb the chair's appearance or seating comfort. Use colorless nail polish to seal the bare metal edges of the newly drilled holes, to prevent rust from starting there.

392 Tip guards for patio furniture

When the metal feet on patio furniture cut through the rubber or plastic tips that encase them, they will create scratches and rust stains on the patio surface. Make each tip last longer by fitting a metal washer inside, against the bottom, so that the leg rests on the washer rather than cutting into the tip.

393 Make-your-own furniture guards

Many pieces of patio furniture, especially folding chairs, rest on metal runners instead of legs. Aside from being noisy when moved, the runners can scratch the patio surface and leave rust stains. Protect both the runners and the patio beneath them by covering them with lengths of old hose slit along the side.

394 Clothesline-to-glow

Did you ever run into your clothesline at night? Eliminate this dangerous possibility for yourself and others by running a sponge full of luminous paint the full length of the line. Let the line remain up until the paint dries. The line will stay brightly visible long after the sun has gone down each day.

395 Discouraging birds

Birds love to perch on the horizontal top rail of an outdoor swing set. This inevitably means bird droppings on the swing, which are not only ugly and corrosive but dangerous to the health of children. Here's how to make the top rail a much less attractive perch. Screw a corner bracket to each end of the rail. Then suspend a long dowel between them with a nail at each end running through a bracket hole and into the dowel. It can then revolve freely, like an axle. As soon as a bird lands on it, it will begin to turn, which will cause the bird to fly away to a more stable perch.

396 No shock outdoors

When you're working outdoors with power tools, the risk of electrical shock is greater than when working indoors. Minimize this risk by using only an extension cord that ends in a ground fault interrupter (GFI) outlet box that you plug the tool into. Or, use a proper size extension cord plugged into a GFI-protected outlet on the exterior or interior of your house. (All exterior outlets should be on GFI circuits, according to the National Electrical Code.)

397 Which side up?

When you're laying the floor of a wooden deck or porch, remember that the boards will be less likely to split if they are installed with their bark side up. To determine which side of a board is (or, rather, was) the bark side, examine the curve of the growth rings at either end. The board should be laid so that these rings arch upward, as if forming a mound.

398 A dry porch or deck

Bothered by peeling paint on your porch or deck? Moisture is probably seeping into the boards from the ground underneath. There are two things you can do to correct the problem: Lay a sheet of plastic over the ground to serve as a moisture barrier, and/or paint both the upper surface and underside of the deck with the same water-repelling enamel.

399 Getting a hold on mold

All kinds of molds and lichens can easily flourish in concrete walls, patios, and walkways. Here are some ways to prevent this from happening: Prune overhanging trees and plants to give the concrete surface better air and light circulation; grade the earth around the concrete so that water drains away from the concrete; make sure that gutters and downspouts are not leaking water onto—or near—the paved surface.

If molds or lichens have already made an appearance, here's how to get rid of them. First, brush the affected areas with a stiff-bristled brush to remove as much of the growth as possible. Then, coat them with a solution of one part bleach to four parts water. Two days later, wash them thoroughly with clean water and a scrub brush.

400 Form fitting

Before pouring a concrete patio or walkway, coat the wooden forms with motor oil (used oil is fine). This will keep the cement from sticking to the forms, making them easier to remove.

401 Fence posts that last

Sooner or later, wooden fence posts will start to rot and give way. Make it later with the help of an old inner tube. As you implant the post, run a length of cut-up inner tube under the bottom of the post so that it will fold and cover the entire below-ground surface of the post. Then lash the protruding top of the rubber securely to the post with automobile hose tape. The result is a tight seal that will protect against moisture seeping into the wood.

402 The better split

A maul will split a log more easily if it hits into the true top end of the log. To determine the true top of a log, check the diameter at each end: the smaller end is almost always the top. You can also check the direction of the limb stubs, which point upward toward the top. If the log doesn't have a definite heart in the center to use as a splitting target (elm logs, for example, are roped like muscles), start splitting slabs off the circumference and work gradually toward the center.

403 Wood-splitting guard

Splitting wood can be a messy and dangerous job unless you take some precautions. The next time you split wood, try setting the logs upright within a stack of two old automobile tires. The tires will help support the logs; they'll also keep split wood from flying away and protect the ax blade from accidental damage when it falls short.

404 Firewood shield

Here's an easy-to-build and very effective shelter for a pile of firewood. Drive two poles into the ground behind the pile—one close to each end. Then purchase or cut a sheet of corrugated plastic that is a few inches bigger than the pile on all sides (a 2x12 foot sheet should do for the average size woodpile). Cut two slots in one side of the sheet for the poles to go through, making each slot a few inches longer than the pole width. After the wood is stacked in front of the poles, put the cover in place on top of the pile. The holes will keep it in place and let it ride down the poles as the wood is removed. Keep one end of the pile higher than the other so the cover will slope somewhat, permitting rain and snow to run off.

405 Hauling help

Hauling bulky furniture or repair and maintenance supplies in your car often requires ingenuity if you want to minimize stress, strain, and avoid accidental damage or loss. Here are some tips for making hauling jobs easier and safer:

• Take a swim float or a couple of old inner tubes with you when you need to haul lumber or a large, flat item on the roof of your car. The float or the tubes can be placed under the cargo to protect the roof of the car and cushion jolts while traveling.

- Carry four large C-clamps, several long lengths of rope, and an old blanket in your trunk at all times. The clamps can be attached to items to be transported, to serve as tie holds when you need to rope items into the trunk or across the roof, and the blanket can be placed around or under hauled items to protect them and the car.

- When you're forced to travel with the trunk lid ajar to accommodate what you're hauling, keep the lid in place with an elastic strap that has a hook on either end (available at hardware, bicycle, or camping stores). Attach one hook to the lid itself and the other hook to the car frame.

406 Lock lubrication

Every six months, the locks around your house need lubrication. You can do this with powdered graphite, but here's another way that's just as good. Take an ordinary soft pencil (No. 1 or No. 2) and rub the point, which is made of graphite, on both sides of the key until it is pretty well covered. Then push the key in and out of the lock a few times. This motion will enable the pencil dust to lubricate the lock.

407 Where to put left-over cement

Once you've opened a bag of cement, the bag itself loses some of its sealing ability, and leftover dry cement may get wet and harden if you store it in the bag. Instead, store leftover cement in an empty coffee can with a tight-fitting plastic lid.

7

PLUMBING, ELECTRICAL, AND HEATING

408 Tighter sink and tub caulking

Many people discover that the caulking around their sinks and bathtubs splits and deteriorates so badly after a couple of years that it needs to be replaced. The caulking around your sinks and tubs will last much longer if you apply it while the sinks and tubs are filled with water. Their filled weight will open up seams to the greatest extent where caulking is to be applied.

409 Tub insulation

When you install a new bathtub, put glass or mineral fiber insulation underneath the tub. It will reduce the noise factor when you're filling the tub, and it will keep the water warm for a longer period of time.

410 A safe drain-cleaning solution

If hot water alone won't clear a clogged drain under a sink, try this drain cleaning solution, which is safe on pipes and won't bother a septic system. After the water in the sink has emptied or been bailed out, pour one cup of baking soda followed by one cup of vinegar down the drain and immediately plug the opening with a closed strainer or a dishrag. Leave the drain tightly covered for 20 minutes, so that the bubbly chemical reaction of the soda and the vinegar has ample time to work on the clog. When the time is up, flush the drain with hot tap water for several minutes.

411 Hot way to declog drains

The most common cause of a clogged drain is grease build-up in the trap. If you suspect this is the case, heat the trap with a portable hair dryer or heat lamp. This should melt the grease, at which point you can run very hot water to clean it out completely.

412 Wire for drain clearing

If you have a clogged drain and a plumbing snake isn't readily available, try clearing the drain with a piece of sturdy wire, such as a coat hanger. Straighten it out, bend the hook in the end a bit smaller, and poke it into the drain repeatedly as far as it will go.

413 Fixing a plunger handle

Does the handle of your plunger wobble or pull out when the rubber cup gets stuck to a surface? Simply slip an adjustable hose clamp around the neck of the cup and tighten it securely around the handle. Use an automobile hose clamp, which resists corrosion.

414 More suction for your plunger

Make your plunger function more effectively by smearing a little petroleum jelly all around the rim of the suction cup. It will give the cup a much better seal and, therefore, much better suction. When you've finished using the plunger, rinse the cup in hot water and wipe it off with a paper towel.

415 Better threads with jelly

After you unscrew the drainpipe under a sink, coat the threads with petroleum jelly prior to screwing it back together. Not only will the connection be less likely to drip, it will be much easier to unscrew in the future.

416 Ready and waiting washers

Replacing a worn-out washer in a leaky faucet is not a difficult job, but finding the right size washer is often a challenge. The next time you have to replace a faucet washer, wire several extra washers of the correct size to the shut-off valve in the water supply line for future replacements.

417 Emergency pipe leak repair

To stop a small leak until you or a plumber can fix it permanently, turn off the water supply and use either of these strategies before turning the water back on

- Cut a small section of split rubber hose (about 4 inches long for a small hole). Slip the hose section around the pipe with the leak in the center. Place a C-clamp or small wrench against the hose directly over the hole and tighten it until the leak stops.

- Cut a strip of inner tube or rubber sheeting about a foot long and an inch or two wide. Start wrapping the strip around the pipe about 6 inches from the leak, stretching it tightly as you go and overlapping half of each previous turn. After you've finished, tie a cord around that end and go backward, wrapping the cord around the rubber strip in half-inch laps. When you reach the other end of the rubber strip, tie the cord securely.

418 Repairing pinhole leaks

If water seems to be seeping from an invisible hole in a pipe, wrap the suspected area of the pipe in several layers of plumbing tape. If you do manage to spot the leak, plug it with a round toothpick, break the toothpick off, and wrap over it. If the hole is slightly larger than a toothpick, but not large enough to warrant a new pipe, close it up with a short, self-tapping galvanized sheet metal screw driven through a small "gasket" piece of rubber.

419 Pipe freeze warning

Pipes running through a crawl space can freeze in cold weather. To monitor whether they're at risk, use an indoor/outdoor thermometer with a remote outdoor sensor. Position the thermometer in some interior space where it can easily be seen (such as a garage, an enclosed porch or a kitchen), and put the remote outdoor sensor near the pipes. Then, if the crawl space temperature dips toward freezing, you can take corrective action.

420 Baseboard security

The pipes carrying the water for baseboard heating systems can freeze if the boiler should break down and the surrounding temperature drops below 32° F. This can be especially troublesome because baseboards use copper pipes, which are inclined to burst when ice forms inside, causing major damage throughout the house. To prevent these lines from freezing, add antifreeze to the water in them before shutting the system down. Be certain that there is a backflow protector, called a check valve, in the water supply line to the heating system to prevent backup of antifreeze into other water lines.

421 Thawing frozen pipes

When you suspect a pipe is frozen and you want to thaw it out, first shut off the main water valve and open all the taps. This will drain most of the system, keeping large volumes of water from gushing out of the pipe once it's thawed. Then feel around the suspect pipe(s) until you find the spot that's colder than any other—that's where the ice is. If the pipe hasn't ruptured there, wrap it with a heavy towel and place a bucket directly underneath. Then slowly pour hot (but not boiling) water onto the towel. The towel will absorb the water and let it surround the pipe for a few minutes, and the bucket will collect the overflow. As an alternative, heat the pipe slowly with a portable hair dryer or a heat lamp, always keeping the dryer or lamp in motion, working back from the faucet toward the frozen area.

If the frozen pipe is a drain pipe, the best way to thaw it out is to pour hot (but not boiling) water down the drain. To get closer to the blockage, remove the trap, put a bucket underneath it, and insert a short length of hose into the pipe until it can't go in any further. Then pour the hot water through the hose with the aid of a funnel, making sure the funnel end of the hose is higher than any other spot where the water will travel, to avoid a backup overflow.

If the frozen spot in a pipe has ruptured, be sure to put a bucket beneath it before you thaw. Then, after thawing it out, make some sort of emergency repair on the pipe itself before reopening the system.

422 Don't pump trouble

If you have a water system in which a pump fills a reserve tank from which water is drawn for use, don't take chances when you leave the house for 8 to 12 hours or more in very cold weather: turn off the power to the pump. That way, if the heating system should fail and a water pipe freeze and burst, only the amount of water in the tank can run out and possibly cause damage. The pump won't start operating when the tank level gets low and create a steady flow of water through the leak.

423 Taking the bang out of pipes

Sometimes after you've shut off a faucet, the water pipes may bang (a condition known as "water hammer"). This can happen even though you have air chambers in your plumbing system that are designed to prevent it. Try this remedy. Turn off the water at its source and open the faucets at the highest and lowest points in your plumbing system. Let all the water drain until all dripping has ceased. Then close the faucets and turn the water back on at its source.

Chances are good that the banging was caused by the air in one of the air chambers leaking out into the pipes and/or by the chamber itself becoming water-logged. By draining the system, you allow the chamber to refill with air.

424 Pipe strap cushioning

When the straps holding a pipe in place are slightly larger that the pipe itself, noisy vibration can occur. To rectify this situation, remove the strap, slip a slit section of old garden hose around the pipe, and reinstall the strap. The grip should then be tight enough to eliminate the vibration problem.

425 Tighter taps

Frequently the copper washer-sleeve inside a compression unit that connects a water tap to its shut-off valve develops a leak even though the nut is very tight. Eliminate this problem by wrapping the sleeve with pipe thread tape and then tightening the nut.

426 Pipe block when soldering

When you're soldering a pipe joint, a single drop of residual water or leaking from the shut off valve can ruin the job. Keep this from happening by stuffing a slice of bread up the pipe above the soldering point. When you finish soldering and turn the water back on, it will break up the bread and carry it off.

427 No-sweat toilets

Bothered by condensation on the outside of your toilet water tank? The best way to solve this problem is to insulate the inside of the tank. First, drain and dry the tank. Then cut a piece of ½-inch rubber or polystyrene foam for each inside wall and several pieces for the bottom of the tank. Glue them in place with silicone cement. After giving the glue 24 hours to dry, refill the tank and resume normal use.

428 The last straw for leaky toilets

Often a leaky toilet is caused by the lift chain getting caught under the flapper valve when it closes. To eliminate this possibility, cut a plastic straw in half and slip the lift chain through it. The straw will settle at the bottom of the chain, keeping it stiff and unable to be sucked beneath the flapper valve.

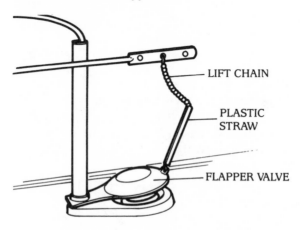

LIFT CHAIN

PLASTIC STRAW

FLAPPER VALVE

429 Toilet water conservation

Flush toilets waste an enormous amount of water. To cut down on the waste, fill two half-gallon plastic containers with water and place them in the toilet tank. This will lessen the amount of water needed to refill the tank, but it won't affect the quality of the flush.

430 When the toilet won't stop

If the water in your toilet won't stop running, here's what to do. First, lift the float ball in the tank. If the water stops running, unscrew the float ball from the float arm and shake it, to find out if there's water inside. If so, replace it. If not, reattach it and bend the float arm down slightly so that the water never rises higher than ¾ of an inch below the top of the overflow tube. If the water still keeps running, close the shut-off valve and replace the entire mechanism in the tank with a plastic ball-cock assembly.

431 When the toilet won't flush well

Your toilet may not be flushing well because the stopper ball returns too soon to the valve seat where the water runs out of the tank. To keep the stopper ball afloat longer, try these steps.

1. Raise the guide arm about ½ inch higher on the overflow tube, if it is adjustable.

2. Bend the top of the upper lift wire so it is a bit shorter and the ball will be lifted a bit higher.

3. Insert the end of the wire in a hole in the lift arm that is closer to the overflow pipe. This will lift the stopper ball even higher.

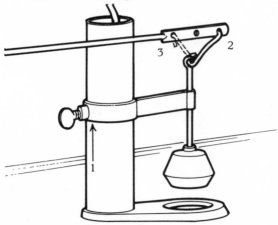

432 When your toilet churns

If your toilet tends to make a churning sound, the tank is only filling partway with water. First, make sure the stopper ball drops squarely onto the valve seat. If it doesn't, turn off the water and flush the toilet to empty the tank. Swing the guide arm until the stopper ball can drop straight down to sit perfectly centered on the valve. Then lift the ball and feel around the valve seat with your fingers. If the surface feels uneven or corroded, sand it smooth.

433 Opening a trap or cleanout

The screw-in plug in the trap or in cleanouts of a main drain line is a flat plate with a square or hexagonal lug protruding from the center for a wrench to grip. What can you do if you want to run a snake through the drainpipe but can't remove the plug because the wrench lug is rounded off from wear? It's a common problem with several solutions:

1. Use a metal file to reshape square corners on the lug. Also, squirt penetrating oil around the threads to make the extension easier to move.

2. File a v notch in the lug, fit a chisel into the notch, and hammer against the chisel so that the lug turns in a counterclockwise direction.

3. As a last resort, break the plug. Use a power drill with a metal twist bit to drill a series of holes in a straight line across the plug, running as close to the center of the plug as possible. Then use a hammer and chisel to break the plug along the line you've drilled.

When you replace the plug, coat the threads with petroleum jelly to prevent corrosion or oxidation that would freeze the plug in place.

434 Clearing drains yourself

Before calling an expensive plumber, try clearing a clogged drain yourself with a hand-powered plumber's snake and water running through a garden hose. Begin by cranking the snake through the pipe. Next, remove the snake and flush the pipe with the hose, running the water at full pressure. Repeat the process if necessary.

435 Cutoff collar

When a pipe bursts or some other plumbing emergency strikes, even the coolest head is likely to panic. To make sure that shutting the water cutoff valve does not present a problem in such times, make a helpful "reminder collar" out of an empty plastic bleach bottle. Just cut the bottom out, make a hole in the center, and fit it over the stem of the valve, under the handle. Then mark a large arrow with a felt-tip pen and label it to indicate the "off" and "on" directions.

436 Ready at the cutoff

Buy an inexpensive wrench that fits the cutoff valve at your gas meter and tie it to the meter with a plastic cord. That way, you can always cut your gas off right away in the event of an emergency. Otherwise, you may waste precious time running to and from your workshop.

437 Shower versus bath

If you're concerned about saving water, remember that it's better to shower than to take a bath. A 4-minute shower uses 50 percent less water than the average bath.

438 Cleaning a shower head

Does an even stream of water come out of your shower head? If not, then some of the holes in the shower head may be clogged. Here's how to get them completely clean again. First, remove the shower head by holding the shower arm with one wrench and using another wrench to unscrew the head from the arm. Make sure both the arm and the head are padded with tape where the wrenches are gripping them. Rinse out the head to remove loose particles of sediment or rust. Next, let the head simmer for five minutes in a 50/50 solution of vinegar and water. Afterward, give it a thorough brushing with a bottle brush. This should remove any lime deposits from the holes. Use a needle or hairpin to poke out any stubborn deposits. Finally, wrap the shower arm pipe threads with Teflon tape and replace the head, using two wrenches as before.

439 Proper hot water setting

Most electric water heaters are set at 140° F. This makes water much hotter than you ever need it to be. Set the temperature at 120° F. instead and you'll notice the savings on your monthly electric bill.

440 Water heater time off

An electric hot-water heater uses a lot of energy. To save money, attach a thermostat to the heater that will switch it off during the night when you aren't using it and switch it on just before you wake up in the morning. Also, turn your water heater off altogether (if possible at the circuit breaker or fuse box) when you leave the house for a couple of days or more.

441 Water heater drainage

To make your water heater operate as efficiently as possible, open the drain cock at the bottom and drain off one or two gallons of water every four months. This will get rid of sedimentary deposits that can interfere with the heating elements.

442 Wintertime bathing

Whenever you take a bath during the cold months, delay draining the tub until the water has cooled off. That way, the water will help not only to warm the bathroom but also to humidify it—reducing the dry air problem that many houses have in the winter, which leads to increased static electricity.

443 Pilot light versus ignition

Many older, gas-fired water heaters still have pilot lights. If your water heater is one of them, replace the pilot light with an electric ignition unit. It's a cheaper and safer method to use in the long run since it only works on demand.

444 Go for the cold water

When it comes to washing clothes, cool water (typically around 80 degrees Fahrenheit) in combination with a cold-water detergent works just as well as hot water for all but the greasiest items. It also saves energy and, therefore, money, cutting the average cost of washing clothes by about one-third.

445 Water pipe insulation

Hot water pipes should be insulated to prevent heat loss. That will cut your water heating bill and give you hot water at the tap faster. Cold water pipes that "sweat" with condensed moisture during hot weather should also be insulated to eliminate this problem. Condensation can cause corrosion and can damage whatever it drips onto.

446 Homemade pipe insulators

You can make pipe insulators that are cheaper and even more effective than the ones sold in stores. Cut 6-inch-wide strips from fiberglass batts that are 3½ inches thick and faced with foil. Wrap the strips one after the other around each pipe, keeping the foil side facing out and securing each strip to the pipe with duct tape. Be sure to wear gloves throughout this entire procedure.

447 Plumbing system

Don't wait for an emergency to decipher the maze of pipes, valves, and meters in your basement. Tie clearly marked baggage labels to the different components of your plumbing system, including the hot and cold water shutoffs, the water meter, the drain cleanout access covers, and the destinations of all pipes. Also, draw a diagram of the system and display it near the entrance to the basement.

448 Avoid soft (water) drinks

If you install a water softener, consider having the cold water line to your kitchen sink bypassed, so it provides untreated water. The sink is the source of all the water you cook with. Water softeners treat the water with sodium compounds, and most Americans need less, not more sodium in their diets.

449 Advice on attic fans

Hot air rises, so it makes sense to open attic and second-story windows when the outside temperature is hot. It makes even more sense to install a fan in the attic to cool the whole house. Attic fans are classified according to how many cubic feet of air they can move in a minute, a measurement designated CFM. To find the right attic fan for your house, calculate the volume of the house (length x width x height, in feet), multiply by 30 (the number of air changes per hour that the fan should make), and divide by 60. For maximum benefit while using the fan, the total open window area on the ground floor, for intake of cooler fresh air, should be about double the area of the fan.

450 Summer storm windows

After winter has run its course, don't remove storm windows (or storm doors) wherever you use air conditioning in the summer. The extra glass barrier helps keep the air-conditioned area cooler.

451 Cross-ventilating

By far the most energy efficient way to cool your house is to set up good cross ventilation. Regardless of how the wind is blowing, the opening of the window on one side of the house or a room should be higher than the opening of a window on the other side. Double-hung sash windows are ideal for this: Just open one from the bottom and the other from the top. The higher opening should be larger than the lower one.

452 Increasing sun protection

Leaving window shades down or curtains closed during a sunny summer day definitely keeps a room cooler, but heat is still getting inside that room through the window glass. A far more effective sunblock is an awning or a shade tree just outside the window.

453 Helping air conditioners

Air conditioners work much better if they don't have to overcome the effect of direct sunlight. If possible, keep your air conditioners out of direct sunlight by mounting them on shaded walls or beneath awnings.

454 Raise high the air conditioner

Trying to decide where to build an air conditioner into a wall? The best place is as near to the ceiling as practical, since the higher you go, the hotter the air will be. Also, putting the air conditioner high lets the cold air flow out across the upper part of the room and drop downward. In addition, try to place an air conditioner in the coldest outside wall so that the condenser unit outside can cool off the coils more efficiently. A northern wall is ideal.

455 Heating system size check

A gas or oil heating system that is oversized for your house will function inefficiently. The system will burn fuel so fast that it will only run for short intervals unless the weather is extremely cold. To determine if your system is oversized, clock when it switches on and off during a cold evening. If it runs less than 40 minutes every hour, its capacity should be reduced. A serviceperson can do this in a number of ways, including changing the nozzle to a smaller size. It's especially important to check if your system is oversized after you've made major improvements in your insulation.

456 Wall insulation inspection

Here are some ways to tell whether your exterior walls are insulated:

- Remove light switch and electrical outlet plates and see if there's insulation around the outside of the terminal box.

- If the framing is open in your basement, look up between the 2x4s on the exterior walls.

- Go inside a closet that's built against an exterior wall, poke a hole in the wallboard with a screwdriver, and shine a flashlight through the hole to see if there's insulation behind the hole.

- Inspect all exterior walls for "ghostlines" where the studs are. Within an uninsulated wall, dust particles accumulate between the wall and the framing, and eventually this accumulation discolors the wall itself.

457 Checking for R-values

Insulating materials are rated in terms of R-values, which differ according to the kind of material and its thickness. "R" stands for "resistance to heat loss;" the higher the value, the more effective the insulation is. What R-values are required for various parts of your house depends on what part of the country it is in. To determine the approximate values needed, refer to the map and chart below.

U.S. Region	Walls	Basement Ceiling	Attic Floor
A	R-11	R-11	R-26
B	R-11	R-13	R-26
C	R-13	R-19	R-30
D	R-13	R-22	R-33
E	R-13	R-22	R-38

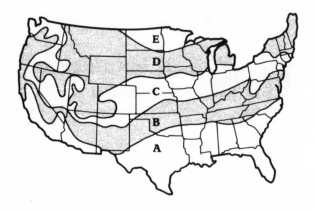

458 Insulation tip

As a general rule, all heating and cooling ductwork, including electrical conduits, in the attic, basement, or crawlspace should be covered with at least 2 inches of fiberglass insulation. This prevents warm or cool air loss through cracks or sudden changes in the surrounding air temperature. When installing the insulation, be sure to wear protective gloves and clothing.

459 A feel for soot

Concerned that your heating system isn't giving you as much heat as it should? Often this is because soot has piled up at the point where the duct turns to enter the chimney. To check out this possibility: When your furnace is on, quickly touch the top of the duct at this point and then quickly touch the bottom directly underneath. If the bottom feels cooler, then soot has collected there and is insulating it. Shut down the system and clean out the soot when the duct cools.

460 Icicle alert

Do you get long icicles hanging from the eaves in the winter? This is a sign that your roof is warm, which could be due to one or more of the following factors:

1 .The temperature inside the house is too high.

2. There's not enough insulation in the attic.

3. There's inadequate ventilation in the attic.

The first problem should be easy to check and alleviate. As for the second, make sure that your attic has at least 6 inches of insulation in the ceiling, extending all the way out to the edges. Checking for the third problem, poor ventilation, involves some calculation. You need 1 foot of screened venting for every 300 square feet of roof area. Half of this venting should be near the very top of the roof and the other half should be along the lower edge.

461 Sealing attic fan louvers

During the winter months, cold air can easily sneak into your home through closed attic-fan louvers. Keep this from happening by taping a removable plastic storm window (available in kit form at hardware stores) over the louvers.

462 A degree of savings

You can even go a littler further during the summer, by setting the air conditioning thermostat at 78° F. During the winter, set the heat thermostat at 68° F. Each degree over 78 in the summer and below 68 in the winter will save approximately 3 percent of your cooling or heating costs.

463 Check thermostat

When you feel that a room is actually hotter than the thermostat is set for, unscrew the thermostat and check the hole in the wall that the wires run through. Often this hole is big enough to allow cold air from inside the wall to get into the thermostat, so it is not sensing the true air temperature in the room. To block the cold air flow, fill the hole with a dab of putty or caulking compound.

464 Heat source clean-up

For proper heat distribution, clean a radiator or baseboard convection unit every 3 months. Turn the radiator or convector off, remove the cover or grill, if any, and wait until the unit is cool to the touch. Then vacuum the radiator sections or the convector fins thoroughly. Finally, rub it with a wet rag or sponge to remove any caked-on dirt.

465 Best radiator color

The best color to paint a hot-water radiator is flat black. Dark colors radiate heat better than light colors, and flat paint surfaces radiate heat better than glossy ones. The difference in heat emission between a flat black radiator and a glossy white radiator (the worst color for radiation) is roughly 10 percent.

466 Homemade heat reflector

To get more heat from your radiator or baseboard convector, make your own heat reflector to insert behind it. Tape heavy-duty aluminum foil to a piece of ¼- or ⅜-inch thick insulation board or foam-core paneling. It should be a few inches wider and, especially, 6 to 8 inches taller than the radiator or convector, if space permits.

467 Let sleeping sediment lie

When you have fuel oil delivered during the heating season, shut down your furnace during delivery and leave it off for 20 to 30 minutes longer. That will give sediment and dirt stirred up by the inflow of the new oil a chance to settle to the bottom of the tank again, so it won't be drawn into the system, where it could cause clogging or faulty operation.

468 Maintaining an oil burner

If your oil bill seems to be creeping higher for no good reason, a poorly functioning burner might be responsible. A technician should examine the carbon dioxide level in the flue. Anywhere between 10 and 13 percent is ideal. If it's less than 8 percent, the combustion chamber may be leaking, there may be an insufficient or excessive draft, and/or there may be an unbalanced air-to-fuel ratio.

469 The bargain of wood heating

To cut down on your wintertime heating costs, consider using a wood stove for part or all of your heat, if permitted in your area. A standard cord of wood (a stack that measures 8×4×4 feet), which is relatively inexpensive, produces as much heat as 146 gallons of heating oil, 17,400 cubic feet of gas, 3,300 kilowatt hours of electricity, and slightly less than 1 ton of coal. A woodburning stove is also not affected by power outages!

470 Removing a broken bulb

When you break a bulb in its socket, it's hard to find a safe place to grasp it and unscrew it for replacement. Try jamming a bar of soap, a large cork, or a piece of raw potato into the base of the bulb and then twisting it. The broken bulb should come out with no problem.

471 Reviving light bulbs

If a light bulb is flickering, it could mean that the terminal on the base of the bulb is dirty or corroded. Try cleaning it with a pencil eraser or with a few strokes of a metal file. The same technique often works with dim flashlight batteries.

472 Keeping bulbs removable

By the time it burns out, a light bulb can be difficult to unscrew for replacement (especially if it's outdoors and more susceptible to oxidation). Avoid this by giving the ridges on the threads of the light bulb a thin coat of petroleum jelly before you install it. Coat only the ridges, not the valleys of the threads, because jelly in the valleys will obstruct the electrical contact.

473 High bulb changer

To avoid having to set up a ladder every time you need to change a hard-to-reach light bulb, make your own "high bulb changer." Remove the bulb clip from an old lampshade and attach it to a broom handle or similar stick 4 to 6 feet long. Wrap the loops of the bulb clip with rubber tape so they will grip the bulb tightly. Slip the clip loops over the overhead bulb and turn the handle to unscrew the bulb. Then put a new bulb in the clip and use the changer to insert it in the overhead socket.

474 A switch with elbow room

Do you find yourself repeatedly entering a kitchen, a workshop, a nursery, a laundry, or some other room with your hands full, unable to flick the light switch until you put things down? Put in a "seesaw" or rocker switch wherever you have this problem. The "on" and "off" ends of the switch are large enough to press easily with your elbow.

475 Extra seconds of light

Don't fumble around in the dark after you've turned out a light. Instead, replace the light switch with a time-delay switch. It keeps the light on for a brief time after you switch it off—30, 45, or 60 seconds, depending on the model.

476 Visible light switch

When you're entering a room at night, you shouldn't have to grope around in the dark to locate a light switch. Aside from being inconvenient, it's also unsafe. Replace the existing switch with one that has a continuously illuminated lever.

477 Easier switch-turning

Many people have trouble turning the round knob of a conventional lamp switch, either because it is too small or because of the lamp's position. To make the task easier, cap the switch knob with a No. 15 (⅜-inch) cane tip with ¼ inch of its length cut off. In most cases it will fit snugly.

478 A rewire relay

The most frustrating part of rewiring a lamp is working the new cord up through the inside of the lamp base. It can be done very easily, however, if you remember to tie a string to the top end of the old cord before you pull it down and out. The string will follow the path of the old cord out and you'll be able to use it to pull up the new cord.

479 Temporary splicing

Sometimes it's necessary or desirable to join the ends of two electrical cords when you don't have soldering tools available to make the connection safe and solid. To provide a temporary splice until you can get the tools (which should be as soon as possible), stagger the ends of the wire pairs so that the splice in one is 2 inches or so from its neighbor. Then insulate the temporary splices with tape.

480 Wet wire stripping

Stripping rubber or plastic insulation from electrical wire is far less tedious if you use a wet knife. Keep a can of water nearby and dip the knife blade into it from time to time as you go along.

481 Cup prop

Holding two wires in position to solder them, or two pieces of thin material to put a drop of superglue in exactly the right spot is a challenge. Give yourself some help with a Styrofoam or paper cup prop. Cut slits in opposite sides of the rim and wedge the pieces you're working on into the slits so that their ends touch over the center of the cup. In addition to being a third and fourth hand, the cup will catch any solder or glue drips. If you need to stabilize the cup, put some sand or water in it.

482 Electrical work with polish

A small jar of fingernail polish can come in surprisingly handy when you're working with electrical wire.

After replacing a plug, keep the wires from fraying and sticking out from under the screws by dipping the twisted ends in fingernail polish before tightening them. If you find a bare spot in an electrical wire and you don't have any electrical tape on hand, turn off the current and seal the spot with a small dab of fingernail polish.

483 From lamp to extension cord

Need an extension cord but don't have one available? Remove the shade from a lamp, unscrew the light bulb, and screw in a plug receptacle. The lamp will function as an extension cord. Do not plug power tools or tabletop appliances into this makeshift extension, however. Lamp cord is not rated for the amount of current tools and appliances draw.

484 Circuit identification

Whether your electrical system uses fuses or circuit breakers, make sure you can tell which circuit controls which outlet(s). Record this information on the inside of the door of the fuse/circuit breaker box. Also, mark the number of the appropriate circuits on the back side of each switch plate or outlet cover. This will help ensure that you turn off the right circuit when you work on that outlet. By putting the labels in plain sight the information will be available for anyone who needs it.

485 Let there be noise

Suppose you're working on an electrical job upstairs and you want to cut off the power to that outlet from the fuse box in the basement. How can you be sure that the power is actually off without having to run back upstairs? Before you go to the basement, plug a radio into the outlet you want to cut off and turn the volume up loud. When you take out the right fuse, the sound will stop.

486 Safe footing

Keep a rubber mat by your electric service entry panel (the main fuse or circuit breaker box). For your own safety, be sure to stand on this mat whenever you operate any controls in the panel. Never reach into a service panel with two hands; keep one in your pocket. Touching anything with one hand while the other touches a hot element in the panel may ground you so that a circuit runs through your body (thus defeating the value of standing on the rubber mat). In addition, it's a good idea to keep a supply of fuses and a flashlight nearby.

487 Hands off pipes!

In many houses, the electrical system is grounded to the water service entrance pipe. Since the entire plumbing system is connected to that pipe, be careful not to come in contact with plumbing pipes when you're working on electrical repair tasks.

488 Beware of conducting pipes

Whenever you're involved in a plumbing repair, take care not to splice any plastic pipe into a plumbing line that also serves as a grounding conductor. Use only metal pipes or pipe sleeves. Otherwise you will break the path to the ground.

489 Insulated gripper for pliers

When working on electrical repairs, insulate your pliers by slipping a 15-inch length of rubber hose over the ends of the two handles. This will also make the pliers more comfortable.

490 Screwdriver insulation

Don't risk accidentally shocking yourself when you're

using a screwdriver on an electrical project. Wrap the shaft from just above the tip up to the handle with electrician's tape. This will prevent a short circuit when the tip touches a hot contact and the shaft accidentally touches a metal object. If the handle has any exposed metal, such as rivets, wrap it in tape, too. And always remember that the best protection of all is to shut off the current to a circuit at the fuse or circuit breaker box.

491 Ground-fault receptacles

Most electrical codes now require that outlets in bathrooms, laundry rooms, kitchen sink areas, and other high-moisture locations have ground-fault interrupter (GFI) protection. This will cut off the power the instant any current leakage occurs, such as from a short circuit caused by water splashed into an outlet or across appliance contacts. Protection can be provided by individual GFI outlets in a given circuit, or by GFI circuit breakers in the control panel. Each breaker will protect all the outlets on its circuit. You may be able to install the outlets yourself, if you have some electrical experience, but installing a circuit breaker is a job best left to a professional.

492 Candles in a storm

During a power failure, a votive candle contained in glass can provide bright, continuous light for many hours and even days. A flashlight will only work for a few hours at best. The flame on a votive candle is also safe from drafts and sudden blasts of wind. Votive candles of this type are widely available in grocery and dime stores.

493 Bobby–pin wire clamps

Fastening speaker or telephone wires to baseboards or rafters doesn't have to involve unsightly and damaging tacks or brads. Instead, use bobby–pin clamps. Clip the crinkled prong of the bobby pin just below the loop or eye of the head. Then hook the wire into the loop of the pin and slide the straight prong into the crack between the baseboard, molding, or rafter and the wall or ceiling.

494 Inlets for outlets

To avoid measuring and cutting errors when you're installing drywall around an electrical outlet, try this technique. First, cut off power to the outlet. Then remove the cover plate and the screws that hold the outlet in the box. Replace them with marker screws, which you make by cutting the heads off similar screws, leaving a threaded shaft about ¾ inch long, and sharpening one end. Install the marker screws with the points facing out. Move the drywall panel into position and push it firmly against the sharp screw ends to make two locator marks in the back. Lift the panel away, align the screw holes of a spare electrical box with the locator marks, and trace the outline of the opening you need to cut for the outlet box.

495 Emergency fuse substitution

If you blow a fuse and don't have a ready replacement on hand, don't worry about missing the big game on television. Just remove a good fuse from another, less critical circuit and use it to replace the blown one.

496 Suction snaking

Running electrical wire through a curved length of conduit can be very frustrating. Here's a trick for making the job easier. First, cut a length of yarn several inches longer than the pipe. Then hold or secure one end of the yarn and suck the other end through the conduit with a vacuum cleaner. Next, tie the secured end of the yarn to one end of a length of stout cord several inches longer than the conduit. Pull the cord through, then tie the cord to the wire at whichever end is most convenient and pull the wire through.

497 Cord guard

It's easier than you may think to accidentally cut through the electrical cord on your hedge trimmer. Prevent this from happening by slipping a 3-foot section of garden hose over the part of the cord that's nearest the trimmer and binding it in place with electrical tape. The hose is too thick to fit into the teeth of the trimmer and will keep the cord from snaking beneath the teeth. This same technique is advisable for many other hand-held electric power tools.

498 Cord coiler

Customize a large plastic bucket or cylindrical cardboard carton so that it can store and feed a long electrical extension cord that you use for different jobs around the house. On the side of the bucket or carton, almost at the bottom, make a hole big enough to allow the pronged plug of the cord to pass through to the outside. Then coil the rest of the cord in the bucket or carton. Whenever you need to use the cord, it will roll out easily as you pull it. When you're finished, it will form easy-to-unwind coils as you drop it back in. You can carry tools or other small items inside the coils in the bucket as you go to or from a job.

499 Clean up metal with magnets

Take a hacksaw or a file to a metal pipe and you're bound to produce metal slivers, which can be irritating and difficult to clean up. With any pipe that's not copper or brass, which are nonmagnetic, try using a magnet wrapped in a piece of plastic kitchen wrap. Run it over the litter. Peel off the wrap over a wastebasket and the slivers will drop into the basket.

500 Wiring with a glue gun

When you need to secure low voltage wiring (such as telephone, thermostat, and doorbell wiring) to walls and ceilings, a hot-melt glue gun can come in very handy. Make a line of glue an inch long and $\frac{1}{8}$ inch wide, press the wire into the line, and hold it there for a few seconds until the glue sets. Repeat this procedure every 2 feet.

INDEX

padding, 30
portable, 29
Vitamin C, 67
Votive candles, 151

Wallcovering, 51, 77-80
Walls
    insulation inspection, 141
    moss removal from, 107
    paneling, 81-82
    patching baseboard, 83
    patching holes, 82-85
    removing mastic from, 102
    smoothing drywall seams, 85
    stud detection, 81
Washer-and-nut bonding, 96
Washers, 129
Washing clothes, 138
Water conservation, 133, 136
Water cutoff valve, 136
Water hammer, 131-132
Water heaters, 137-138
Water softeners, 139
Weathering, paint and, 61
Weatherstripping garage doors,
    116
Wet mowing, 117
Wet wire stripping, 148
Wheel-stoppers, 115-116

Window boxes, swinging, 108
Windows
    cleaning, 88
    cracked glass, 88
    opening stuck, 86-87, 89
    pane removal, 107-108
    patching screen, 108
    reviving frames, 107
    security for, 87-88
    storm, 139-140
Winterizing garden tools, 118
Winter seeding, 118
Wintertime bathing, 137
Wire-pinning, 10
Wiring (see Electrical work)
Wood heating, 145
Wood preservative, 67
Wood rot, 102
Wood splitting, 124-125
Workbench
    drawer, 9
    fold-away, 8
    grounding metal, 10
    mat, 7
    top, 7
    wire-pinning, 10
Workshop, 7-18
Wrenches, 32

Yardsticks, 39-41